FAMILY THERAPY WITH SCHOOL RELATED PROBLEMS

James C. Hansen, Editor
Barbara F. Okun, Volume Editor

The Family Therapy Collections

AN ASPEN PUBLICATION®

Aspen Systems Corporation
Rockville, Maryland
Royal Tunbridge Wells
1984

616.89156

F21F1

#10299218

Library of Congress Cataloging in Publication Data
Main entry under title:

Family therapy with school related problems.

(The Family therapy collections, ISSN 0735-9152; 9)
Includes bibliographies.
1. Family psychotherapy. 2. School children—Mental health.
3. Child psychotherapy. I. Hansen, James C. II. Okun, Barbara F.
III. Series. [DNLM: 1. Family therapy. 2. Students—Psychology.
3. Schools. WM 430.5.F2]
RC488.5.F355   1984   616.89'156   83-25758
ISBN: 0-89443-609-0

Publisher: John Marozsan
Editorial Director: Margaret Quinlin
Executive Managing Editor: Margot Raphael
Editorial Services: Ruth Judy
Printing and Manufacturing: Debbie Collins

The Family Therapy Collections series is indexed in
Psychological Abstracts and the PsycINFO database.

Library of Congress Catalog Card Number: 83-25758
ISBN: 0-89443-609-0
ISSN: 0735-9152

Printed in the United States of America

1   2   3   4   5

Table of Contents

iii

Board of Editors

Contributors

BARBARA F. OKUN, PhD
Coordinator, Family Systems Therapy Program
Northeastern University
Boston, Massachusetts

JOAN S. ANDERSON, PhD
Private Practice
Houston, Texas

ZOILA AVILA-VIVAS, MA, CAGS
Doctoral Candidate
University of Massachusetts
Amherst, Massachusetts

MARGARET S. BAGGETT, PhD
Private Practice
Atlanta, Georgia

JANINE M. BERNARD, PhD
Purdue University
West Lafayette, Indiana

DON DINKMEYER, PhD
President, Communication
and Motivation Training Institute
Coral Springs, Florida

JAMES DINKMEYER, MA
Associate, Operations Manager,
Communication and Motivation
Training Institute
Coral Springs, Florida

PHILIP GUERIN, MD
Center for Family Learning
New Rochelle, New York

JAMES C. HANSEN, PhD
State University of New York
at Buffalo

ARTHUR M. HORNE, PhD
Professor of Counseling
Psychology
Indiana State University
Terre Haute, Indiana

DAVID KANTOR, PhD
Director, Kantor Family Institute
Cambridge, Massachusetts

ARLENE KATZ, EdD
Family Institute of Cambridge
Cambridge, Massachusetts

LUCIANO L'ABATE, PhD
Director, Family Psychology
Program
Georgia State University
Atlanta, Georgia

GISELA MORALES-BARRETO, MA
Doctoral Candidate
University of Massachusetts
Amherst, Massachusetts

ANNE PERETZ, MSW
Executive Director,
The Family Center
Somerville, Massachusetts

Contributors

(continued)

CELIA SPACONE
State University of New York
at Buffalo

ENA VAZQUEZ-NUTTALL, EDD
Associate Professor
University of Massachusetts
Amherst, Massachusetts

JOHN M. WALKER
Doctoral Fellow
Indiana State University
Terre Haute, Indiana

ROSAMUND ZANDER, MSW
The Family Center
Somerville, Massachusetts

Preface

The Family Therapy Collections, published quarterly, are designed primarily for professional practitioners. Each volume contains articles authored by practicing professionals, providing in-depth coverage of a single significant topic of family therapy. This volume focuses on family therapy initiated because of concern with school-related problems.

The family and the school are the two most significant systems in a youth's life. The family is the primary influence in the development and socialization of children. Children learn early patterns of behavior, communication, expression, values, and attitudes from the nuclear and extended family members. Later, the school not only develops cognitive skills, but also influences the youth in terms of social and emotional behavior. The youth continues to be affected by interacting in both systems. Since most referrals for family therapy concern a youth as the identified patient, therapists are clearly involved in the interaction of these two systems.

When working with a school-related referral, the therapist must identify the specific problem and the variables that contribute to it, such as physical factors of the child, family interactions that could stimulate or maintain the problem, or conditions in the school. The therapist must be knowledgeable about the school system, as well as about family dynamics, in order to intervene adequately. Working with school personnel to gain information about the child in that setting, the therapist may implement an intervention in the school. This volume presents concepts and techniques to use in working with families around school-related problems.

Dr. Barbara Okun, Associate Professor of Counselor Education at Northeastern University and Coordinator of the Family Systems Therapy Program, is the volume editor. In addition to being an educator and practitioner in family therapy, she has authored and edited numerous books and articles in the field. Dr. Okun has selected skilled therapists to contribute articles that will be useful for therapists who work with school-related problems in family therapy.

James C. Hansen
Editor

Introduction

Family therapists in both the public and private sectors receive many referrals of youngsters who exhibit some type of school-related problem, whether it be behavioral, cognitive, or affective. In fact, the family therapist is often the "last resort"; the youngster has been seen by the school psychologist or by an individual therapist in the community, and the problem has not been resolved. In such instances, even though they may be reluctant to participate in therapy, parents feel obliged to cooperate because of their extreme concern about their youngster's functioning in school and because of their exasperation and frustration with previous attempts to work through the problem. Thus, family therapists with a systemic understanding of both family and school systems may be in a unique position to effect change by altering system structures and communication patterns in both these major social systems rather than by treating the youngster as a self-contained organism.

The articles in this volume discuss the theoretical bases for intervention strategies that have been successful with families who must deal with school-related issues. My own introductory article focuses on the assessment of a youngster's school-related problems in the context of both the family and the school systems and on the interaction of the family therapist with these two systems.

Luciano L'Abate, Director of the Family Psychology Program at Georgia State University, and Margaret Baggett and Joan Anderson, both private practitioners, demonstrate the necessity of using both linear and circular solutions for families with school-related problems. They propose clear phases of therapy for those cases in which family therapy is deemed the appropriate modality of treatment.

Philip Guerin, Director of the Center for Family Learning in New Rochelle, New York, and Arlene Katz of the Family Institute of Cambridge, Cambridge, Massachusetts, propose an assessment model for the child-centered family that takes into account the triangle of family-school-child. The transcript of an actual case is used to illustrate their points.

James Hansen, Professor, State University of New York at Buffalo, and Celia Spacone, a doctoral fellow, present a systems view of a child with a learning disability and present a case study to demonstrate the dynamics of the family of such a child.

The three subsequent articles focus on special populations. David Kantor, Anne Peretz, and Rosamund Zander of The Family Center, Somerville, Massachusetts, describe their work with housing project families, focusing on the systemic cycle of poverty and its implications for assessment and treatment. Ena Vazquez-Nuttall, Zoila Avila-Vivas, and Gisela Morales-Barreto of the University of Massachusetts, Amherst, Massachusetts, delineate the challenges that Latin American families present to family therapists and highlight the cultural factors that affect treatment of any culturally different client population. Janine Bernard at Purdue University, West Lafayette, Indiana, discusses the interaction of divorced families and the schools, noting the concerns and issues that family therapists need to consider when working with families in the process of divorce or adapting to divorce.

The two final articles focus on particular theoretical approaches to working with families around school-related issues. Don Dinkmeyer and James Dinkmeyer discuss the Adlerian approach, and Arthur Horne, Director of Training in the Department of Counseling Psychology at Indiana State University, Terre Haute, Indiana, and John Walker, a doctoral fellow, present a social learning approach. These two approaches were selected because of their extensive use by school mental health workers.

It is hoped that these articles will enhance the understanding of clinicians about the reciprocal influences of the family system and the school system and that this heightened understanding will be reflected in the assessment and treatment of youngsters exhibiting school-related symptoms. Consideration of cultural, ethnic, economic, and political variables must be incorporated into every clinician's theoretical formulations.

Barbara F. Okun
Volume Editor

1. Family Therapy and the Schools

Barbara F. Okun, PhD
Coordinator, Family Systems Therapy Program
Northeastern University
Boston, Massachusetts

FAMILY THERAPISTS HAVE BEEN TRAINED TO VIEW INDIVIDUALS' symptoms in the context of their family system and to interact actively with the family system. In fact, major family therapists (Haley, 1976; Minuchin, 1974; Satir, 1967) stress the importance of such interactions between the therapist and the family system to help the family change and function more adaptively, thus alleviating the identified patient's symptoms.

Many family therapists who practice outside of school settings (i.e., in community agencies or private practice) see families referred to therapy because of a child's symptomatic behavior in school. There is little in the literature, however, on the family therapist's interactions with the school system, a major social system in a youngster's life, or on the interactions between the family and school systems. For years, counselor educators have been exhorting school counselors and psychologists to get out of their offices and into the school system itself in order to conduct more outreach programs and to achieve systemwide results. Now it is time for the family therapist to get out of the office and into the school system. The therapist must consider a child's symptomatic behavior within the contexts of both the school and the family in order to understand the meaning and implications of the behavior and to arrive at effective interventions.

From a systems perspective, a child's symptoms reflect the stresses and strains within the school or family system, or between these two major systems. This model takes into account all the primary interactions in a child's life and the ways in which the child's symptomatic behaviors both affect and are affected by the behaviors of those around the child. These symptoms may be present in one or both systems, in similar or dissimilar forms. Because the child's primary interactions occur in both the family and school systems, it is necessary to include both systems in a total assessment process.

OVERVIEW OF SYSTEMS THEORY

A family system and a school system are organizational structures. Each is a "system composed of a set of interdependent parts" (Okun & Rappaport, 1980), and a change in one part of the system effects change in other parts of the system. Because a system itself has basic needs to adapt, survive, and maintain itself, it takes action and behaves. Systems are fluid, ever-changing. When the needs of the component parts (an individual member or a subsystem) conflict with the goals of the total system, the system attempts to regulate and control the behavior of the component parts.

2

Control of the system is maintained by its structures and by its cybernetic principles of communication and feedback.

All human social systems consist of smaller groups of people, called subsystems. Alliances and coalitions form within and among these subsystems. In families, for example, there are sibling, couple, and parent subsystems; in school, there are classroom and grade subsystems, to name a few. Both overt and covert rules, determined according to the system's power structure (direct and indirect), govern the interactions of system and subsystem members. Every system assigns roles to its members. Some allow for negotiation and change of these role assignments, and some do not. Systems have evolving or established problem-solving practices and communication patterns and styles. The boundary permeability between and among members, subsystems, and the total system determines the rigidity or flexibility of interactions not only within the system, but also with other social systems. Each social system and each subsystem within it influences its members and is, in turn, influenced by its members to varying degrees and intensities.

System Similarities and Differences

Although the family and school systems both have a major impact on a youngster, there is no doubt that the family system's influence on a child is more personal and pervasive than that of the school system. Membership in each system is different for a child. The child's membership in the family system shapes the family's natural evolution into a functioning organization over time. Important factors that affect this process include the couple system dynamics, how and why the decision was made to have the child, the couple's experience of pregnancy and childbirth, the ease or difficulty of the child's early infancy, and the child's impact on the economic, social, and physical resources of the family. By the time the child enters a school system, the child has already been significantly socialized by the family system in terms of learned roles, behavioral rules, communication styles, and interactions. This child is expected to join and adapt readily and immediately to the established school system, which, of course, reflects the larger community system.

Membership in a school system is not voluntary, as it is required by law. Children are assigned to a major subsystem of a school system, a classroom, which may or may not resemble the structure of their family system. The classroom is a transitory subsystem that develops and dissolves over the course of just 10 months. Then the children enter a new and totally different subsystem, repeating the adaptation and classroom socialization process over and over again for 12 years. As children pass into junior and senior high school, they may have to adapt to several competing, different subsystems within the course of 1 day.

It is not uncommon for a child's family system style to clash with the classroom system style. A child raised in what Kantor and Lehr (1975) called an "open" family system is accustomed to decision making by consensus and a democratic power structure in which different points of view are expressed and considered. If this child is assigned to a "closed" kindergarten classroom, the child may have difficulty adapting to a more authoritarian power structure in which clear and unnegotiable rules are set and opposition or discussion is discouraged. The child may be labeled a problem child as he or she struggles to adapt to the new environment and to the teacher's expectations. This label may follow the child through the child's school career, setting the stage for school-related problems of various sorts. In actuality, the problem is a systems clash—the youngster has not yet learned the skills necessary for adaptation to various system styles. Understanding different system styles makes it clear that the child's difficulties are adaptive rather than pathological.

According to systems theory, the individual does not have a fixed personality or traits, but acts and reacts in response to contextual cues. A child may, for example, behave one way at home and another way at school. Furthermore, at home the child may behave one way with one parent and another way with the other parent, just as at school the child may behave one way with one teacher and another way with another teacher. Different teachers often have strikingly different perceptions and interpretations of the same child's behavior. Again, the child's behaviors must be viewed in relationship contexts.

It is important to focus on the interactional patterns and sequences within and between family and school systems to see how a problem is maintained in a particular system and how these two major systems influence each other to maintain the child's problem. An advantage of this focus is that no one person is considered responsible for a child's difficulties. Everyone in the system contributes in some way, and changes can occur at differing places in varying forms.

Kinds of Problems

Family therapists treat four broad categories of problems: (1) systems incongruency, (2) developmental disorders, (3) nondevelopmental disorders, and (4) external crises.

Children bear the brunt of any incongruency between the value system of the family and that of the school. This is particularly true for children whose families are outside the middle-class mainstream of society for whom public schools are oriented. Children from nontraditional families and from minority groups are continuously struggling with the different attitudes and expectations of their family and school systems, and they find it difficult to accommodate to the competing systems. Families may encourage individuation; schools, conformity. The family may value sports over academic pursuits; the school, vice versa. The family has a definite effect on a child's school performance (Goldenberg & Goldenberg, 1981), and a major goal of therapy may be to improve the congruency between the family and school systems.

Developmental problems may arise when either the school or family system is unable to adapt or change in accordance with the family life cycle or the school year cycle. The stresses and strains that occur as a system passes from one stage of development to the next can lead to dysfunction (see Duvall, 1977, and Okun, 1984). In the family life cycle, for example, developmental stress may be associated with separation issues as the family enters the school age stage and the child leaves to enter a nonfamilial major influence system (the school), or with the difficulties experienced as the family moves into the adolescent stage and family power and other resources must be reallocated. Developmental stress in the school year cycle may result from the need to adapt to a new teacher and peer group at the beginning of the school year (i.e., new rules, roles, and expectations), prevacation excitement, or termination anxieties at the end of the school year.

Problems may also stem from nondevelopmental crises in either the family system or the school system. Although such crises cannot be considered part of normal family or school development, they appear with considerable frequency, affecting the parents' and teachers' interactions with children. It is not at all unusual for children to begin to exhibit learning or behavioral problems in school just when family tensions are peaking from divorce, family violence, alcoholism, or a major illness. Likewise, teachers who are undergoing stress and strain from their own divorce or family crisis often find their perceptions of and style of relating to students heavily taxed by this crisis.

External crises also affect either the family system or the school system. A child's father may lose his job, or the family's home may be burglarized, resulting in heightened anxiety and behavioral dysfunction in the child. A school committee's refusal to ratify a teacher's contract, fear of a reduction in force or the implementation of new policies, or the inauguration of a new administration can strongly affect the morale, self-image, and behaviors of classroom teachers; this, in turn, affects the entire classroom system. Any of these crises is likely to impair system functioning. Boundaries may become blurred, and levels of differentiation may drop. When levels of differentiation are low, normal processes used to distinguish between intellect and emotion are inhibited, and this can result in inappropriate behaviors in children and in overreactions in parents and teachers. Crises heighten anxiety, which may cause a parent dyad or school personnel dyad to triangle in a child to reduce the dyad's anxiety (Bowen, 1978) or may cause a particular individual to over- or underfunction for the child. When tension and anxiety increase beyond the level that the two person or party system can manage, a third person—usually the most vulnerable, least well-differentiated person in the system—is recruited into the two person or party system to lower and diffuse anxiety and tension. For example, if mom and dad are worried and fighting about their son's low grades, it may be safer for them to triangulate in the teacher, blaming him or her for unfairness or incompetence. In this way, they can join as spouses, lessen their anger with their son, and alleviate the family tensions and fighting.

ROLE OF THE THERAPIST

As stated earlier, in order to assess a referred problem accurately, the family therapist must actively join with both the school and family systems. Without a complete and accurate assessment, it is difficult to formulate realistic goals and effective intervention strategies. Because the family therapist is not a member of either system, the therapist is in a unique position to focus on the welfare of the child; with no vested interest in either the family or the school system, the family therapist is in an invaluable position to offer useful, credible consultation to both. This consultation can be educational as well as remedial.

The amount of disengagement between the school system and the mental health community is surprising and frustrating (McDaniel, 1981). As long as they remain disengaged, chances of sustained improvement with a school age child diminish. As parents within a family system need to improve their communication in order to facilitate effective parenting, so do significant others within the school system, family system, and mental health profession need to improve their communications with and understanding of each other's interactions with the child.

The family therapist must join with each major social system, but must not become part of a particular alliance or coalition. The therapist must establish credible rapport in a supportive, nonthreatening manner with the people who comprise the power structure (the influencers) in each of the two systems. The family therapist can serve as a conduit, a bridge, between these systems. The same strategies and styles used to join with the subsystems within a family system can be used to approach these two major systems as interacting subsystems of an even larger social system, the community. If a community agency, such as a welfare or guidance clinic or the courts, has been steadily involved with the client family, it is necessary to include the significant personnel of this agency in the assessment and treatment processes. The family therapist then becomes a coordinator as well as a consultant to all the major social systems involved with the child. The therapist's task is not to function as expert parent or teacher, but to mobilize the system's resources so that parents can parent more effectively and teachers can teach more effectively.

Data are collected by direct observation, by interview, and by the assignment of direct tasks. The therapist must be careful not to prejudge, judge, or blame. The child's problem(s) must be presented in a way that engages the family system, the school system, and any other major system that may be involved in collaboration and cooperation so that these systems will support the intervention strategies selected to address the problem.

Obviously, the family therapist is in a unique position to provide feedback to both systems. This must be done without violating the privacy or confidentiality of any party, however. For example, if the family therapist learns that the child's problem behavior in school reflects the strain of the parents' decision to divorce, the therapist must be careful not to share this information with the teacher unless the parents so request. Instead, the family therapist could suggest to the teacher that the child is perhaps not receiving adequate attention at home and is attempting to compensate for that in school. By helping the teacher understand the motivation for the child's classroom behavior, the therapist may be able to help the teacher differentiate personal feelings from thoughts regarding the child and interact with the child in a different way. The therapist may be able to suggest some behavioral strategies that would reward the child with attention for appropriate behaviors and ignore inappropriate behaviors.

Assessment

The family therapist must consider the reciprocal influences of the family and school systems and the possible impacts of these influences on the child in order to understand fully the child's behaviors in terms of transactions and relationships within subsystems and the larger systems. Without assessing the degree of congruence between the operating rules of the family and those of the school system, without evaluating information provided by both parents and teachers regarding the child, and without actually observing the child in both the family and classroom settings, the therapist will overlook important data.

It is important for the assessment process to include at least one session attended by every member of the family system. This is usually the first session. At this meeting, the therapist can obtain each person's perspective of the problem, observe firsthand the child in the family context, and join with the family and engage its members in collaborative work. The types of information that may be sought include

- how each person perceives his or her place in the family (in, out, peripheral)
- what each person believes to be his or her unique contribution to the family (e.g., Dad the economic provider, Mom the nurturer, Billy the tease, Mary the good girl)
- what each person believes to be the problem in the family (sometimes family secrets emerge)
- who each person believes hurts the most in the family (often this turns out to be the person most bothered by the problem, not the identified patient)
- what each person would like to change about the family
- what each person believes to be his or her greatest strengths in the family
- how the identified patient's problems affect each member of the family
- how long and in what way these problems have existed
- why the family has come for help at this particular time
- what has been done in the past to attempt to deal with the problems

The therapist may also explore the family's developmental stage, the external and developmental stresses operating at the time of treatment and at the onset of the problem, levels of differentiation within the system, and operating triangles, particularly those involving the identified patient.

This information may be elicited through verbal techniques, such as questioning or responsive listening; individual or group draw-a-picture techniques; family sculpting (each family member in turn arranges the family in a tableau that shows the sculptor's perceptions of system and subsystem members' relatioships); or any other strategy that works for the therapist. The goal of this assessment is to engage the family in treatment and reframe the child's problem in a way that helps the family members to view it as a system problem and to commit themselves to resolving the problem together. As systems resist change, this is no easy task!

The goal of classroom observation is to see firsthand how the child interacts with the teacher and peers, to evaluate the congruence between the child's needs and the teacher's expectations, and to determine the contextual factors that contribute to and maintain the child's inappropriate behaviors. In addition to observing the child in the classroom and other school activities, the therapist should elicit from school personnel the following information:

1. each person's perception of the child's problem at school
2. the person for whom the child's behavior is the greatest problem
3. the duration and form of the current problem
4. the child's strengths and weaknesses
5. the efforts that have been made to date to correct the problem
6. the approaches recommended by different school personnel
7. the result that would show school personnel that the problem had been solved
8. the strengths and resources of the school that may be used to help the child

After the family and school assessments have been made, it is helpful for the therapist to meet in conference with family, school personnel, and representatives of any involved agency. The purpose of this meeting is to provide feedback that will help the group understand the child's problem from a systems perspective and engage in collaborative intervention strategies. Such meetings also help to bridge the gaps between the systems by improving communication and problem-solving patterns.

The following example shows the necessity of both a school and family assessment in order to understand the nature of a child's problem behavior:

Ralph, age 7, was referred to a family therapist by the school psychologist because of his underachievement, inattention in class, poor peer relationships, and inappropriate talking during lessons. The school psychologist and Ralph's mother were at loggerheads; the former was blaming the latter for poor home discipline, which she believed carried over into the classroom, and Ralph's mother felt that school personnel were unfairly picking on her son.

The family therapist's first meeting with Ralph and his divorced parents provided important family information. Ralph had been in treatment at a local guidance clinic since his parents' divorce 4 years earlier; this "patient" role kept his parents in constant communication with each other, preventing their emotional separation, and resulted in triangulation over discipline issues with Ralph at the apex of one triangle involving his parents and another involving his mother and the school. Because Ralph spent every weekend with his father in a downtown high-rise apartment, he missed necessary peer socializing experience; thus, his peer relationship skills were underdeveloped. As the sole focus of each parent's attention, he was accustomed to getting his own way most of the time, and he felt more comfortable with attentive adults than with other children. He had developed effective manipulative strategies to manage his parents, and he was puzzled as to why these strategies did not work as well with his teacher at school.

A visit to Ralph's classroom revealed other significant data. As the family therapist entered the school building, she was met by the principal and the school psychologist, who carried a very thick file about Ralph. The principal's first comment was "Oh, I'm so glad you've come. Ralph is the most disturbed boy in this school, and we all worry so much about him." Already, Ralph's role as the school system's identified patient was evident.

The family therapist observed in the classroom that Ralph was indeed singled out for discipline more frequently than other boys whose behavior was even more disruptive. Later discussion with the classroom teacher indicated that the observed behavior was typical and further emphasized the teacher's enmeshment with Ralph and her determination to keep him in the identified patient role. The therapist also found out that the teacher was in the process of a painful divorce herself and that she was experiencing enormous anxiety about the effects of her divorce on her 7-year-old son. She expressed fear that her son would end up "disturbed like Ralph."

Thus, the family therapist learned that both the school psychologist and Ralph's parents were right. Home discipline was inconsistent, and Ralph was picked on unfairly in the classroom. The therapist's major goals were to relieve Ralph of his learned patient role and to teach him more effective peer relationship and teacher relationship skills. This was accomplished by (1) working with the parents to provide more consistent discipline and management at home, as well as clearer boundaries; (2) working with the school psychologist and classroom teacher to provide similarly consistent discipline and management at school and to restructure the classroom boundaries. Simultaneously, the family therapist was able to establish a trusting rapport with the classroom teacher and refer her for divorce counseling. Ralph's mother and teacher developed a working alliance that improved congruency between home and school operating rules, and Ralph was helped to differentiate his relationship with each of his parents in separate father-son and mother-son sessions. The therapist served as a coordinator and consultant. Ralph's immediate behavior improvements reinforced the cooperation of the family and school systems.

Goals

The family therapist must select goals that are feasible and manageable, alleviate the problem(s), and lead to sustained system development. After determining how systems had been operating and what led to their breakdown, the therapist can select the appropriate intervention. Rather than restore the system functioning to its previous level, the therapist hopes to help recalibrate the system to a newer and higher level of functioning that incorporates new patterns and structures, and allows the system to remain viable, fluid, and able to adapt to continuous change.

Thus, goals may be short-term, intermediate, and/or long-term. They focus on interactions and relationships within and among systems, and they must be expressed in behavioral terms so that it is clear when the problem has been solved, when change has occurred.

Interventions

There are as many different approaches to working with families as there are family therapists. The task of the family therapist is to determine where, when, and how to intervene in each case. Interventions may focus on (a) the child, (b) the child-teacher relationship, (c) the child-peers-teacher relationships, (d) the child-teacher-principal or outside resource person relationships, (e) the child-teacher-parents relationships, (f) the child-parents-school counselor relationships. Several different interventions focusing on more than one treatment unit may be utilized simultaneously. Any intervention strategies that are suitable to the particular problem and are within the therapist's realm of expertise can be useful. There is no one way to treat any problem, and the systems perspective allows any number of effective access points and intervention strategies.

Whenever possible, it is helpful to involve both parents and teachers in intervention strategies. Such strategies may include behavioral contracts requiring the cooperation of all significant parties; periodic conferences with the teachers, the parents, and the child; increased or decreased involvement of the parent in the child's homework, as appropriate; cooperative support of the child's participation in special programs, such as a school group for children of divorcing parents; or special needs programs. Useful interventions are intended to improve communication styles and relationships so that individuals and systems can adapt and cope with inevitable stresses and strains and learn more effective problem-solving and conflict resolution skills and strategies.

CONCLUSION

Collaboration of parents, school personnel, and family therapists requires energy, time, and effort from people already overburdened with commitments and responsibilities. It is important to identify the benefits of such collaboration in order to facilitate the process of joint work. Viewing a child's problem as the result of system dysfunction makes it possible to take a more holistic approach to the child's problems and to achieve more permanent results as the family and school systems' interactional patterns improve.

If a family therapist is able to join with both the family and the school systems for just one case, the lessons learned in the process may be helpful to the family's other children and to many other children in the classroom. A school visit is well worth the cost of 3 or 4 hours of therapy. The results may be more profound in terms of prevention or early remediation than the family therapist ever imagined.

REFERENCES

Bowen, M. *Family therapy in clinical practice*. New York: Jason Aronson, 1978.

Duvall, E. *Marriage and family development* (5th ed.). New York: Lippincott, 1977.

Goldenberg, I., & Goldenberg, H. Family systems and the school counselor. *The School Counselor*, 1981, 28(3), 165–178.

Haley, J. *Problem-solving therapy*. San Francisco: Jossey-Bass, 1976.

Kantor, D., & Lehr, W. *Inside the family*. San Francisco: Jossey-Bass, 1975.

McDaniel, S. Treating school problems in family therapy. *Elementary School Guidance and Counseling*, 1981, 15(3), 214–223.

Minuchin, S. *Families and family therapy*. Cambridge, MA: Harvard University Press, 1974.

Okun, B. *Working with adults: Individual, family and career development*. Monterey, CA: Brooks/Cole, 1984.

Okun, B., & Rappaport, L. *Working with families: An introduction to family therapy*. North Scituate, MA: Duxbury Press, 1980.

Satir, V. *Conjoint family therapy* (2nd ed.). Palo Alto, CA: Science and Behavior Books, 1967.

2. Linear and Circular Interventions with Families of Children with School Related Problems

Luciano L'Abate, PhD
Director, Family Psychology Program
Georgia State University
Atlanta, Georgia

Margaret S. Baggett, PhD
Private Practice
Atlanta, Georgia

Joan S. Anderson, PhD
Private Practice
Houston, Texas

A CHILD'S SCHOOL-RELATED PROBLEM BEHAVIOR MAY RANGE FROM educational underachievement, which may be caused by a variety of learning disabilities, to a host of emotional difficulties, which may be manifested in school in a wide variety of ways (e.g., excessive timidity; withdrawal; inability to make friends; aggressive, attention-seeking behavior; and inappropriate reactions to teacher and peers). If referrals do not come from the school, it is doubtful whether families will allow themselves even to acknowledge that such a problem exists.

THE IMPORTANCE OF EVALUATION

Although an initial evaluation may render the child the identified patient of a dysfunctional family system (L'Abate, Weeks, & Weeks, 1978), a thorough evaluation is necessary before the therapist involves the whole family. What may appear at first to be a systemic disorder may in some cases be related to specific, definable learning deficits. Overlooking these deficits to achieve a family orientation would be as irresponsible as treating the child without considering the family system.

Some may argue that, even if the child is learning-disabled, the disability should be considered within the context of the family. This is not a defensible position, however. It is difficult to change the focus of therapy from the child to the family after the child has been accepted as "patient." Furthermore, when the problem has been identified initially by the school, it is especially important to have evidence to support a family approach. One way to circumvent this dilemma is to see the family first, for one session, as part of the diagnostic evaluation. Another solution is to inform the family at the outset of therapy that one or more family members or the entire family may be invited to attend therapy sessions.

John, aged 11 and in the fifth grade, had a high IQ and functioned above the 85th percentile on group-administered tests. Nevertheless, his grades had been poor, he had not completed assignments consistently, and he had often disrupted the class. His messy papers, as well as his adamant refusal to rewrite them neatly, had been viewed by his teachers and his parents as evidence of his uncaring attitude. John read well and could converse precociously on many subjects, abilities that offered further evidence of his wasted potential ability. The school had given the family an ultimatum: they had to obtain counseling for John, or

14

they had to find another school. The parents chose the first alternative, and the counselor requested a full psychological-learning battery of tests. The results validated the school's test data, with one minor exception. It was found that John had significant graphic expressive deficits. His fine motor coordination was so poor that, although John was 11, his handwriting was not yet automatic, and his quick mind moved so much faster than his hand that utter frustration was the result.

Writing was torture for John, a fact not apparent from group tests in which the "writing" task is confined to blackening small circles with a pencil. John *could not* produce neat papers, especially when he was also attending to other aspects of learning, such as the complicated calculations of a math problem or the orderly dictation of the history teacher. In the lower grades, John had been given more latitude and more time; in the fifth grade, however, the requirements of written work had increased substantially.

John had been labeled with any number of pejorative—and incorrect—adjectives: lazy, uncaring, messy, and emotionally disordered. Worst of all, he had accepted these labels and even added another—dumb! With explanation of the problem to parents, teachers, and John, and with proper remedial help and compensatory techniques in the classroom, John was able to participate in his own recovery. Eventually, by learning to type, he became an excellent student with an outstanding classroom attitude. John's problem was solved by the proper identification and remediation of his learning disability. No family therapy was necessary.

A learning disability that is amenable to educational tutoring (as is usually possible) should be considered at the outset. There must be some evidence to support individualized remediation of the problem "inside" the child or family therapy "outside" the child (L'Abate & Curtis, 1975). Critics may raise questions about the kind of evidence needed in these cases. If, however, a complete history is coupled with a thorough psychological evaluation that includes, in addition to an evaluation of intellectual and emotional functioning, tests of visual-motor functioning, auditory-language functioning, and educational achievement, it is indeed possible to determine whether the problem behavior is related to a specific learning deficit or to an emotional deficit. This is an understudied area that overlaps special education, clinical child psychology, pediatric neurology, and family systems. It is an area that should be confronted much more responsibly by those family therapists who, eager to apply a favorite approach, ignore or bypass deficits that are amenable to more relevant and specific treatment.

LINEAR TASKS FOR LINEAR PROBLEMS

Most problems that appear in the practice of clinical child psychology and family therapy are straightforward and should be treated that way. After a learning disability or other child-related sources of problems have been eliminated, solutions can usually be reached from a family therapy perspective.

Sleep Problems

Many young children have problems associated with bedtime. These may become especially troublesome around age 4, "the nightmare age," when the child is understandably reluctant to trade the security of parental presence for a solitary chamber inhabited by monsters under the bed and ghosts in the closet. When sleep finally comes, dreams about those creatures may cause fitful and interrupted slumber. In this case, the parents should attend the child in the child's own bed until he or she feels able to go back to sleep. The phase will pass as quickly as it came. Little boys, however, may have some resurgence of this behavior around 8 or 10 years of age, as may girls or boys who have experienced some major trauma.

Sleep problems seem to be more prevalent in children whose rooms are at the front of the house, exposed to street lights and noises, or whose rooms are distant from and out of hearing range of the parents' room. Nevertheless, parental treatment is the same. Under no condition should the child be allowed to enter the parents' bed or room. Sleeping with a sibling, an animal, or favorite toys may help. Time is the best cure.

After children reach 8 years of age or so, sleep problems suggest an inadequate parental coalition. For instance, the mother is often in charge of putting the children to bed at night and getting them up in the morning. If the father is present and is less involved in the problem, he should be instructed to see that the children get to bed by a mutually agreeable time. Both parents, together, should convey the message that they will not tolerate a refusal to go to sleep at night and that they will ignore a child who gets out of bed and leaves the room.

Therapists should help parents understand how they reinforce a child's behavior by reacting to it (L'Abate, 1973). Parents should be taught how to assume a less reactive and a more conductive stance (L'Abate, 1983) toward this and other behavior problems; i.e., parents must determine what behaviors they will accept and by what means the acceptable behaviors will be reinforced, instead of merely reacting to the child's inappropriate behaviors.

Parents should also be instructed to avoid the situation in which one of them plays the role of rescuer or even subtly suggests to the child that the other parent's typically sterner approach is not acceptable. The ability to control a parent is frightening to a child. Under such conditions, who will protect the child? The circularity of the situation is obvious.

Parental Neglect

It is always important to assess from the outset how affection is demonstrated among family members, especially between parents and children (L'Abate, 1975). If too little hugging and kissing are occurring, the therapist should prescribe hugging on a regular basis (at least once a day), with the child reporting to the therapist whether the parents are following the prescription.

With recalcitrant teen-agers who reject hugging from their parents, affection may be shown in other ways, such as providing well-liked foods, being available for carpooling, and fulfilling (within the confines of good sense) the teen-ager's need to be a peer clone. The teen-ager must not be allowed to manipulate the parents by pushing them away and thus proving the incorrect hypothesis that either the parents are unloving or the teen-ager is unlovable. The parents must show affection and must understand that rejection from the teen-ager is a developmental stage, not a terminal sentence for inadequacy. Furthermore, the parents must realize that this very distance and independence allow a child to become an adult. As the parents continue to be in control of themselves and their household, they are a source of strength and love into which the adolescent can tap as the youngster's stage permits.

Reading and Learning to Read

Although comic books may be "trashy" and overly violent, they deserve further attention as a way of motivating children to read (Mitchell & Milan, in press). If a 6- or 7-year-old child who is not reading at all has no obvious learning deficit or emotional upset, it may be useful to ask the child to look at a comic book and then either tape-record (another powerful motivator for children) thoughts about the story or tell them to one or both parents. As a reward for either looking at or reading a comic book, the child receives another comic book. It is important that the child be given the freedom to select the comic books *regardless of how the parents feel about them.*

Another way to motivate a child to read is to encourage the child to select material that is interesting but easy to read. The self-concept of "a reader" is better developed if the child easily completes ten 8-page books than if the child struggles through one 80-page book. Because reading ultimately involves writing language, nonreaders can be helped by a family note system by which letters among family members promote interest in decoding exciting information.

Household Chores and Responsibilities

In the area of household chores and responsibilities, the therapist needs to determine how the parents demonstrate power, defined as a combination of authority (who makes the decisions) and responsibility (who carries out the decisions). If the child's noncompliance is related to a tyrannical or indiscriminately rigid disciplinary practice or to a very lax, permissive, often chaotic and inconsistent disciplinary practice, the therapist must strive for a happy medium between those extremes.

The major issue is the age of the child. A 5-year-old cannot be required to be Cinderella any more than a teen-ager can be allowed to escape responsibilities altogether. Written contracts that concern such responsibilities as dressing, room cleaning, and other household chores may be useful. Any contract or agreement needs to define grounds for clarification of issues, negotiation for problem solving, and implementation of solutions.

A 17-year-old, Mary, who adamantly refused to clean her room, insisted that it was "her territory" and "off limits" to her parents. The issue became a source of daily contention in the family. Mary finally ran away (to her grandparents), saying that she would return home only if her parents agreed to allow her to keep her room as she wished. Overcome by fear and feeling helpless, her parents acceded to her demand. Mary returned home, but she became more and more abusive to her parents as time went by. Living with Mary's constant threat to leave, her parents allowed themselves to be victimized by Mary's infantile, controlling behavior; finally, to everyone's great surprise, Mary made a suicidal gesture and was hospitalized.

In the family therapy that ensued, Mary's parents were able to see how their fear had caused them to abdicate their responsibility and had given Mary, a basically good person, an unwanted weapon with which to wound them. Mary had become increasingly depressed, as she interpreted her parents' behavior to mean that they did not care about her. When her parents, in a united stance, were finally able to tell her that she had a choice of cooperating at home—including cleaning her room—or moving out, she immediately chose to stay and to cooperate. Other issues were explored in therapy, but the crisis was over. As soon as Mary was willing to assume her share of the family responsibilities, she again felt like a member of the group and therefore could be accorded some voice in its functioning.

Weak Parental Coalition and Unbalanced Power

Power should be shared. As democratic and equitable as this principle may be, it must be implemented by some specific procedures.

Forced Holding

In some cases, a hyperactive child has been given the power to defeat the rest of the family directly or indirectly, verbally or nonverbally. Either by commission or omission, parents have allowed themselves to be supplanted by the child in the leadership role. In such a situation, the less involved parent should be encouraged to restrain the child (Johnson, Weeks, & L'Abate, 1979*). The first phase of this restraint involves the child's anger and ensuing attempts to test the strength of the restraint. The parent is instructed to place the child on his or her lap and to put one leg over the legs of the child; embracing the child, the parent holds both of the child's hands so that the child cannot move. The child is then informed that "Daddy and Mother are the bosses in the family." The child must repeat this rule while looking straight into the restrainer's eyes, without laughing.

Initially, the child will try to wriggle out of this hold and try to bite or hit the restrainer (eyeglasses, earrings, pens, and pins should have been removed). In the second phase—wearing out—the child continues to test the consistency and strength of the restraint by struggling to regain control and force the parent to let go. When the child realizes that this is indeed a congruent message ("I mean what I say, and I say what I mean"), the child will begin to cry. After this catharsis, the child should be able to acknowledge in a serious manner who is the boss. The parent following this procedure should be prepared and have the physical stamina to restrain the child, sometimes for as long as 20 to 30 minutes.

Sudden Leaving

In most functional families, parental departure is preceded by appropriate, timely notice to the child about the times involved and the nature of the activity. Such information gives the child a sense of security and provides a

---

*This description of forced holding is an update of that in the original publication.

model for behavior as the child begins to engage in social relationships. The parents then leave on schedule, paying no attention if the child whines or tries in other ways to manipulate them to stay; the parents return when promised or before. If, however, the parents have become caught in the machinations of the child who not only throws a tantrum when they leave, but also continues to act as the authority while they are gone, other methods may be indicated.

At a workshop in 1981, Mara Selvini-Palazzoli and Guiliana Prata suggested the following procedure as one way to define generational boundaries between parents and children. After the babysitter has come and has been properly instructed, the parents depart without telling the child where they are going, what they are going to do, or when they are returning. If the child is still awake when they come back, the parents should resist any demands for explanation or description of their activities. Before using this approach, however, parents should be certain that they are spending enough time with the child at home and that they have established themselves as trustworthy and responsible adults.

Rules for Adolescents

When the parents of an adolescent are unable to join together in the decision-making process and, essentially, to use power together, the adolescent may exploit the situation. Two major rules can be instituted to resolve this problem as part of the family conference process (L'Abate, 1981). All the adolescent's activities that involve the parents in some way (e.g., driving, delaying meals, money) must be approved by *both* parents at the *same* time at least 24 hours before the activity is to take place. When the adolescent's request is made at the last minute and only one parent is present, an automatic no is mandatory, regardless of the merits of the request. If the parent asked accedes to the request, thus undermining the absent parent, the absent parent is (if there is time) to disagree and to deny the request.

These rules allow parents to see that they are not working together and that the teen-ager is exploiting the parents' inability to join forces in decision making. Parental discussion (in the presence of the adolescent) about their individual agendas for child-rearing usually makes the parents clearly aware that the adolescent's behavior is a systems failure in which they all collaborate to bring about dysfunctional behavior. Adherence to these two rules is usually sufficient to stabilize the system and to prompt the family members to learn more creative ways of relating to each other (L'Abate, ms. in preparation).

Going on Strike

Another maneuver to redistribute power in the family when power is not in the hands of those who have most of the responsibilities is the strike. In the typical case of this kind, the wife/mother has most of the family responsibilities and feels ignored, unappreciated, and even discounted by the rest of the family. The husband/father and children resist family therapy because they have the most to lose; their efforts are directed toward maintaining the status quo in which the wife/mother may be no more than a maid/servant. Under these conditions, going on strike can be a powerful maneuver in the struggle to equalize authority and responsibility.

Going on strike must be a carefully planned procedure. It should not be implemented until every possible ramification has been considered, including the rage and anger that it will produce in the rest of the family. Details about the strike procedure should be given to the wife/mother in writing. For example, she may announce 1 week ahead of time that she will go on strike (e.g., as of Monday morning at 7 A.M.). She will not get up to prepare breakfast for anybody in the family. She will not shop for food for the family. She will not cook except for herself; she will not do laundry for anybody except herself; she will not chauffeur anybody; and she will not clean any room in the house except her own. She will not pick up anything for anybody. She will take care of herself, *but no one else!* The striker must be careful to make the announcement without anger, but consistently and congruently. The rest of the family will believe, of course, that going on strike is absolute madness and that the wife/mother may need "help."

Such a strike brings the rest of the family to the negotiating table, ensures that all the family chores and responsibilities are evenly shared and distributed, and leads to regular family conferences. Not until there is a written contract, detailing exactly what and how much each family member will contribute to the family's workload, should the strike be discontinued. A strike that is carefully planned and executed will bring resistant family members into therapy.

Family Conferences

The rationale, content, and process of family conferences are well-known (L'Abate, 1981). Family conferences should be the outcome of any family therapy; that is, after completing therapy, families should have the tools to negotiate most issues, and such negotiation should take place in family conferences. If this goal is not achieved, the ultimate success of family therapy is questionable.

Homework

Most typically, homework problems relate to refusal to do the homework, poor work habits, refusal to take responsibility for studying, or underachievement (once it has been established that the child is of at least average intelligence and is not learning-disabled). Whatever these problems may indicate about the family system (e.g., weak parental coalition, inconsistent discipline, avoidance of overt conflict), the therapist must grapple with them before confronting the whole system. Homework is dealt with by giving the full responsibility for it to the child. Often, one (or both) of the parents is helping the child with the homework and is assuming responsibility for it. Here, the general principle applies: learning and loving do not mix! Unfortunately, some teachers encourage parental involvement in the homework process. The therapist may ascertain the teacher's position not only by listening to the parents, but also by obtaining their written permission to check with the teacher.

Homework should be managed by definite schedules and contracts independent as much as possible of rewards or punishments. Learning is a responsibility; if the parents jointly fulfill theirs, the child will fulfill his or hers. If TV, go-carts, video games, possessions, and money are involved in the process, they can become distractions. They must be clearly controlled to avoid any suggestion of bribery. Where bribery is, blackmail will follow!

Achievement

The compulsive, driven overachiever needs attention just as much as the underachiever does. Of course, responsibilities must be fulfilled; however, the child must be allowed to be a child, and performance must not be used to attack personality. The importance of unconditional love—regardless of the child's performance in school—must be stressed.

CIRCULAR TASKS FOR COMPLEX PROBLEMS

When assigned linear tasks fail because the family is unable or unwilling to do them, a more roundabout (i.e., circular) approach may be necessary. The failure to perform or complete assigned tasks in itself reveals something about the severity of the problem. When linear tasks do not improve systematic behaviors, the therapist must follow circular procedures, such as (a) positive reframing of the symptom, (b) prescription of symptomatic behavior, (c) ritualization, and (d) systematic linkage to the other family members (Weeks & L'Abate, 1982). For instance, the therapist can describe a child's problem behavior as protection for a depressed parent. Instead of recommending or prescribing the undesirable behavior, the therapist must allow the child to speak about the many behaviors that can protect the depressed parent. The child is praised for being so "sensitive" to the parent's depression. No aggressive, violent, or harmful behavior should ever be prescribed. Some resistant behaviors are often better approached circularly.

Temper Tantrums

The most straightforward way to deal with temper tantrums is for the adult to leave the room immediately; temper tantrums do not take place in a vacuum. Unfortunately, this approach is not always feasible because the child follows the adult wherever the adult goes. Consequently, it is better to relabel the temper tantrum as "letting off steam" and sometimes as "being loyal to the adult caregiver," who may have modeled such behavior. Once labeled, temper tantrums should be planned for once or twice a week, with a specific place and length of time (e.g., in the bathroom for 15 minutes by the timer). The parents should then order the child to have the temper tantrum at the prearranged place and time.

Jeff, a foster child who was 10 years old and in the fifth grade, was having temper tantrums in his foster home and at school. During these temper outbursts, he verbally and physically attacked adults and children in an apparently uncontrolled manner. A program was developed at school to give Jeff time to "cool down" emotionally before confronting the situation that had provoked his anger. He was assigned beforehand (i.e., when he was not angry) a place where he could go until he regained control. In other words, he was taught to use delay techniques, a linear intervention.

At home, once a week at a certain time, Jeff was to have a temper tantrum in a specific place while his foster parents observed and encouraged him to release his anger. Boxes and other materials that could not be harmful to him and that he could not harm were available to Jeff during this time. It was explained that it was all right for him to be angry but that hitting people was unacceptable. Furthermore, because he seemed to have a great deal of anger, he could express it through tantrums in the directed manner.

During the first session in which he was to express his anger according to the prescription, Jeff halfheartedly hit or kicked a box or two. On learning of this behavior, the therapist expressed disappointment that Jeff had not tried harder and encouraged him to do better next time. For two more sessions, Jeff was asked to have temper tantrums, but he refused to do so. At school and at home, his anger appeared to subside; he did not attack adults again, although he continued to have fights with his peers (not, however, as frequently as he had before the prescribed tantrums). When the adults controlled his tantrums, Jeff lost the power he derived from his explosive behavior and, therefore, had no reason to continue his outbursts of anger.

These prescriptions change the direction of the sequence that precedes the behavior and, thus, the context of the symptom by putting the patient in charge.

Enuresis and Encopresis

A general principle of paradoxical psychotherapy (L'Abate, in press-a, in press-b; L'Abate & Kearns, submitted for publication) is that if an individual does not control a symptom, the symptom will control the individual. Consequently, achieving control of a symptom means joining it (as a friend) rather than fighting it (as a foe). To give a patient the illusion of control and, eventually, the ability to master the symptom, a therapist should follow the guidelines already mentioned (i.e., positive reframing, and ritualized and systemic prescription). Both enuresis and encopresis are relatively easy to control, provided, of course, that every possible physical cause has been eliminated. These behaviors are especially easy to control when no other dysfunction is visible in the family.

Buffy, a beautiful 8-year-old in the third grade, was referred for therapy because of stealing and lying incidents at school. Psychodiagnostic evaluation revealed that her intellectual ability was in the superior range, but that she was suffering from a visual-motor learning disability. She was a middle child whose two siblings were tough competitors. Also, Buffy had been wetting her pants during the day (not at night), not completely emptying her bladder, but leaking urine over time so that she was able to conceal the wetting except for the odor. Medical examination did not reveal a physical cause for this behavior.

Again, a multilevel intervention was planned. The family was seen in therapy as part of the diagnostic evaluation. Afterwards, Buffy was seen individually, although she was accompanied by her parents for at least part of the session every other time. The learning disability was approached directly through tutoring. In therapy, the parents were helped first to express their anger and disappointment concerning Buffy and then to encourage and compliment her on her assets (which appeared to have been overlooked up to this time). Because the parents had already "tried everything" and failed, Buffy was approached paradoxically to diminish or eliminate her enuresis.

The therapist assured Buffy that it was all right to wet her pants because she was not quite ready to terminate this behavior. Therefore, Buffy was told to continue to wet (these instructions were novel to her and implied that *she* could decide when to stop the wetting), but she was to do so in a manner that kept the wetting a secret from her parents. As Erickson (Haley, 1976) so frequently did, the therapist shifted the focus from the symptom to the performance of the symptom, thus ritualizing it and changing the original reasons (Madanes, 1981) for the symptom in the first place. To change the focus, the therapist instructed Buffy in a boring and elaborate monologue how to keep her parents from knowing that she had wet her pants. Immediately upon wetting her pants, Buffy was to go to her bathroom, rinse them out, hang them to dry in a safe place, and then put them in the laundry.

In addition, the therapist instructed Buffy to keep a simple chart of the number of times she wet and the number of those times that the wetting was detected. The next week, Buffy wet three times, but only once were her parents aware of it. During the next 2 weeks, she wet once, but no one knew about it. Then she stopped wetting. The therapist expressed her surprise that Buffy had decided to stop wetting so soon and stated that she expected some backsliding because she was not yet convinced that Buffy had made this decision once and for all.

Accompanying the discussions about wetting were conversations in which Buffy related her feelings of inadequacy in the family and in the classroom. The therapist dealt linearly with these issues. Within a couple of months, Buffy's parents were expressing their delight in the changes they saw in their daughter. Buffy seemed to be much happier. She was proud of herself because she had controlled the wetting and because her spelling papers were displayed for excellence on the board at school. The lying and stealing gradually ceased without having been dealt with, except tangentially.

Sibling Rivalry

The paradoxical approach is also useful with the symptoms of sibling rivalry. The therapist may say, "You really must love each other a great deal because we only fight with those we love. Therefore, it is important that you continue to set each other off. However, I want you to do it once a week (twice a week) and at prearranged times, for example, as soon as you come back from school (before going to bed) for at least 30 minutes. Father (Mother), I want you to remind them to do it, set the timer, and let them go at it." When the children no longer control the sibling rivalry, it no longer serves a function for them.

Defeating Behavior

Any behavior that results in an incomplete, frustrating transaction, one in which nothing is accomplished and from which bad feelings result, is defeating. This behavior is characteristic of hyperactive children (Smith, Smith, & L'Abate, in press). In addition to paradoxical letters (L'Abate & Farr, 1981; Weeks & L'Abate, 1982), a combination of linear and paradoxical approaches has been found more useful than either approach alone. The family is asked to describe in writing how each member defeats and is defeated by the others. After each has made such a list, a family conference is called to make a master list of defeating behaviors. It is at this point that the therapist may provide a positive reframing: "The defeats are needed by this family to help you stick together. They are the glue that holds this family together. I am scared to think what would happen to this family if you were unable to defeat each other. Consequently, you'd better go on defeating each other." The therapist should specify space, time, and frequency (Kochalka & L'Abate, in press).

CONCLUSION

For every problem, there is a solution; for many problems, there is a series of sequential solutions. Both linear and circular solutions are necessary. In addition, the therapist must keep in mind that symptomatic relief and conflict resolution comprise only the first phase of family therapy. The second phase consists of instruction in appropriate negotiating skills that can be used at home in family conferences and will spread to dysfunctional behaviors that were not otherwise touched in the course of treatment. Eventually, most family therapy must deal with issues of intimacy (the third phase). A 3- to 6-month follow-up is mandatory to check on maintenance of gains (L'Abate, ms. in preparation).

REFERENCES

Haley, J. *Problem-solving therapy.* San Francisco: Jossey-Bass, 1976.

Johnson, J., Weeks, G.R., & L'Abate, L. Forced holding: A technique for teaching parentified children. *Family Therapy,* 1979, *8,* 177–186.

Kochalka, J., & L'Abate, L. Distance, defeats, and dependence in family systems: Descriptive and explanatory concepts in family therapy. In L. L'Abate (Ed.), *Handbook of family psychology.* Homewood, IL: Dow Jones-Irwin, in press.

L'Abate, L. Psychodynamic interventions: A personal statement. In R.H. Woody & J.D. Woody (Eds.), *Sexual, marital, and family relations: Therapeutic interventions for professional helping.* Springfield, IL: Charles C. Thomas, 1973.

L'Abate, L. A positive approach to marital and familial intervention. In L.R. Wolberg & M.L. Aronson (Eds.), *Group therapy, 1975: An overview.* New York: Stratton Intercontinental Book Corp., 1975.

L'Abate, L. The role of family conferences in family therapy. *Family Therapy,* 1981, *9,* 187–192.

L'Abate, L. Styles in intimate relationships: The A-R-C model. *Personnel and Guidance Journal,* 1983, *61,* 284–293.

L'Abate, L. Paradoxical techniques: One level of abstraction in family therapy. In G.R. Weeks (Ed.), *Promoting change through paradoxical therapy.* Homewood, IL: Dow Jones-Irwin, in press. (a)

L'Abate, L. The paradoxical treatment of (marital) depression. *International Journal of Family Therapy,* in press. (b)

L'Abate, L. *Systematic family therapy.* In preparation.

L'Abate, L., & Curtis, L. *Teaching the exceptional child.* Philadelphia: W.B. Saunders, 1975.

L'Abate, L., & Farr, L. Coping with defeating patterns in family therapy. *Family Therapy,* 1981, *9,* 253–265.

L'Abate, L., & Kearns, D. *The tenets of paradoxical psychotherapy.* Manuscript submitted for publication, 1983.

L'Abate, L., Weeks, G., & Weeks, K. Of scapegoats, strawmen, and scarecrows. *International Journal of Family Therapy,* 1978, *3,* 89–99.

Madanes, C. *Strategic family therapy.* San Francisco: Jossey-Bass, 1981.

Mitchell, Z.P., & Milan, M. Imitation of high-interest comic-strip model's appropriate classroom behavior: Acquisition and generalization. *Child and Family Behavior Therapy,* in press.

Smith, M.T., Smith, M., & L'Abate, L. Hyperactivity in children from a systemic perspective: Implications for treatment. In L. L'Abate (Ed.), *Handbook of family psychology.* Homewood, IL: Dow Jones-Irwin, in press.

Weeks, G., & L'Abate, L. *Paradoxical psychotherapy.* New York: Brunner/Mazel, 1982.

3. The Theory in Therapy of Families with School Related Problems: Triangles and a Hypothesis Testing Model

Philip Guerin, MD
Center for Family Learning
New Rochelle, New York

Arlene Katz, EdD
Family Institute of Cambridge
Cambridge, Massachusetts

THE FAMILY WITH A CHILD EXPERIENCING SCHOOL-RELATED PROBLEMS is one subtype of what can be classified as a child-centered family. In clinical practice, the child-centered family by definition is a family in which a child is the symptom bearer. The child's symptoms may take the form of an emotional dysfunction, physical dysfunction, or a relationship conflict. The designation child-centered is one category in a systems-based typology of families developed by Philip Guerin at the Center for Family Learning in which the symptom is viewed as an expression of systemwide dysfunction through its most vulnerable member, the symptom bearer (Guerin & Gordon, 1984). The purpose of the typology is to help organize and clarify the conceptualization of the family process around a particular type of clinical presentation. Symptom relief is the first priority, but it is viewed as Stage One in a more comprehensive approach to the multigenerational family process that produced the symptom.

The assessment of the child-centered family involves obtaining a thorough and precise genogram, determining the synchrony of the symptomatic child's temperament with the family's expectations, and defining the key triangles in the emotional process surrounding the symptom (Ferber, Mendelsohn, & Napier, 1972; Guerin & Pendagast, 1976; Pendagast & Sherman, 1979). A family with a school-related problem usually involves one or more of the following five factors:

1. The symptomatic child is emotionally vulnerable in the family system, and this vulnerability is being played out in the child's peer network or in school, rather than within the family.
2. There is an explicit conflict between the symptomatic child and a school authority figure, most commonly the teacher.
3. There is a covert conflict between the child and one or both of the parents that has been displaced into a conflict between the child and the teacher.
4. The symptomatic child has a special relationship with the teacher that makes the child a target of some unfavored powerful students within the classroom. This represents the school yard version of the classic child triangle.
5. The child is caught up in a triangle based on a conflict between a parent and the teacher. This triangle may be explicit or covert. The child reacts by exhibiting problem behavior, usually of an antisocial or underfunctioning academic nature.

RELATIONSHIP TRIANGLES

In family psychiatry, the concept of a relationship triangle is used to describe, study, and experiment with the emotional process in a set of three interconnected relationships. A number of clinical investigators over the past 25 or 30 years have stated that the triangle forms the basic structural building block of any relationship system. It is important, for purposes of understanding, to make a distinction between the triangle as a structure and the process of triangulation.

The triangle is a structure formed from a reactive, emotional process involving three people. The process that goes on within that triangle is the process of triangulation. If the configuration in that structure is altered, the process is altered, and vice versa.

Two basic mechanisms predominate in the initiation of triangulation. In the first, one member of a dyad moves away from the other and connects with a third person in order to calm an internal emotional upset or to gain an ally in a conflict. In the second mechanism, a third person (often a child) who is sensitized either to anxiety in one member of the dyad or to the intense relationship conflict automatically moves in to settle the upset or becomes caught up in the conflictual process.

Triangulation has long been a central concept of family systems therapy (Bowen, 1966; Fogarty, 1975; Guerin & Guerin, 1976; Minuchin, 1974; Satir, 1967). There are several key triangles that the therapist should consider in dealing with the child-centered family: the primary parent triangle, the parent-sibling triangle, the sibling subsystem triangle, the parent-child-teacher triangle, and the intergenerational triangle. Each of these triangles is pertinent to the family with school-related problems.

Primary Parent Triangle

The father, mother, and symptomatic child comprise the primary parent triangle. Structurally, this triangle usually appears as an overclose relationship between the symptomatic child and the mother, with the father in the outside position distant from both his wife and child. The process and structure, however, may vary. Furthermore, the designation of an overclose relationship between mother and child does not mean a calm emotional connection. Most often, the symptomatic child is sensitized to the level of upset and anxiety in the mother and vice versa. As the mother's anxiety escalates and her state of emotional arousal increases, the emotional tension is transmitted to the symptomatic child. As the child's anxiety increases, it is converted into some form of problem behavior.

Several additional mechanisms may come into play. For example, the child may be sensitized to the father's level of upset, although this is a less frequent pattern and most commonly occurs with fathers and the oldest daughter. The child may develop symptoms as a result of sensitization to either an overt or an underground conflict in the parents' relationship. The child may become the target of the parent in the outside position, usually the father. This targeting may result from the outsider parent's negativity toward the target child because of the child's specialness to the other parent. The child may also become targeted through the distant father's irritation because the child upsets the mother and leaves the father to deal with an upset wife, which pulls him back from his distant position.

Parent-Sibling Triangle

The symptomatic child, a sibling, and one parent make up the parent-sibling triangle. In this configuration, the symptomatic child is usually the insider child (i.e., the child with the favored relationship with the parent). This child may become the target of an older sibling who feels less valued and manages these feelings by applying relationship pressure to the favored sibling. This type of triangle may occur in any family constellation with at least two children, but it is perhaps most often seen in a single-parent family.

> Joan, a single mother of three girls, sought therapy for a school behavior problem in Ginny, her youngest child. Family sessions revealed Joan to have a special relationship with Ginny, one in which she worries about her a great deal and spends an inordinate amount of time with her. Ginny is fiercely loyal to her mother and withholds herself emotionally from Jack, her nonresident father. Amy, the oldest sister, is a physical and behavioral "clone" of Jack; she is negative about her baby sister. Sue, the middle daughter, appears to operate fairly well in all of the different factions of the family and floats free of both covert and overt conflicts.

In the majority of single-mother households, the mother must leave home daily to work. This creates a leadership vacuum at home that, in most instances, is filled by the oldest daughter, who takes over the head-of-the-household position while mother is away. (This can also be true, of course, in dual-career two-parent households, but the phenomenon tends to be less dramatic in these cases.) The oldest daughter, thus, may be in a difficult position. Not only does she assume considerable responsibility without any real power, but also she must vacate the position when mother returns and go back to being "just one of the kids." When the oldest daughter in this position also has a specialness to the absent father, there is a high degree of potential conflict between the mother and the oldest daughter. The conflict most often takes the form of increasing criticism of the oldest daughter by the mother. There is a double standard of conduct, one for the oldest daughter and one for her younger siblings. The oldest daughter keeps her distance from her mother, expressing her negativity in passive-aggressive ways toward her mother and in openly punitive ways toward her younger siblings, especially the mother's favorite child.

Consequently, in these families, symptoms often develop in the youngest child. If family intervention takes the form of increasing the mother's focus on the youngest, the child's symptoms will become worse because pressure from oldest daughter to youngest sibling will increase in response to mother's behavior. If, on the other hand, the intervention is focused on bringing the conflict between mother and oldest daughter to light and deintensifying it, the sibling pressure will be removed from the youngest and the child's symptoms will disappear.

Sibling Subsystem Triangle

The symptomatic child and two siblings may form a sibling subsystem triangle with the symptomatic child most frequently in the outsider position to a close relationship between two siblings. The sibling subsystem triangle deserves investigation in any child-centered family. One of its most important characteristics is its cohesion-fragmentation "index," which indicates the degree to which siblings are emotionally connected or distant from one another. A simple way to assess this index is to ask the children how often they band together behind closed doors to "bad-rap" their parents. Siblings in families with a well-functioning, cohesive sibling subsystem will enthusiastically endorse that activity, while those that are part of a fragmented system will not.

A fragmented sibling subsystem is seen most frequently in families with anorexia, severe behavior disorders, and psychotic level process. The symptom-bearing child is invariably the one in the outside in these triangles among siblings. Parents may strongly resist the inclusion of the better functioning, symptom-free children in the family therapy sessions. When this happens, the therapist must take the position that the other children must participate and may even temporarily isolate the sibling subsystem from the parents by working with the siblings alone in some sessions in order to increase sibling connectedness and alter the dysfunctional sibling triangles.

Parent-Child-Teacher Triangle

In its most common form, the parent-child-teacher triangle is the result of a displacement of a parent-child conflict to the teacher-child relationship. This process is often characterized by a dramatic difference between the child's home and school behaviors. The reactivity of the child to the parent, usually around the issues of control and authority, is exhibited in school. If the involved parent and teacher join forces in "shaping up" the child, the problem behavior escalates. In fact, one way to make this covert triangle explicit is to recommend the joining of parent and teacher, and observe the behavior of the child. This may be done both inside and outside the session. Many teachers are willing to participate in family sessions. After this triangle has been demonstrated to the therapist's satisfaction, the nontriangled parent can be directed to take over the functions of parenting and dealing with the school and teacher; this can have dramatic results. Another technique that is useful in demonstrating the covert parent-child conflict calls for the child to reverse problem school behavior and acceptable home behavior. The therapist does this by suggesting to the child that, as an experiment, she try shifting school behavior to the home and home behavior to the school in a structured way—perhaps on Tuesdays and Thursdays.

There are two other major patterns in the parent-child-teacher triangle. In one variation, the parent has a conflict with the teacher, either because of personality mix or because of educational methods, and the child acts out the parent's feelings toward the teacher. This variation is common when the parent is a professional, especially a teacher. In the other variation, the child triggers an emotional reaction in the teacher that is programmed from another aspect of the teacher's life. In this situation, if the parent too readily joins the teacher, the teacher's "fix" on the child will be missed and the problem behavior, be it behavioral or academic, will increase. The resolution of this pattern often requires involving the administration of the school to assist the teacher in seeing the emotional triggers and the resultant "fix" on a particular child.

THE MODEL

The hypothesis-testing model is based on the notion of tracking, which has previously been used in clinical research to increase awareness of pattern (Katz, 1978, 1981). The major function of tracking is to assist therapists in their developing ability to detect pattern within a system. Tracking is a method of studying the process of the family and the therapy developed by Guerin and Fogarty at the Center for Family Planning in New Rochelle, New York. Tracking can be defined as an observational commentary on a consultation or a therapy session in which two processes are monitored and explained: (1) the flow of movement in the family itself and (2) the interaction between the family and the therapist. In the past, what each clinician has tracked has been affected by his or her frame of reference, belief system, and theoretical bias. The hypothesis-testing model allows the clinician to track pattern in a more objective manner.

The hypothesis-testing model is a formalization of the process wherein the therapist makes observations, becomes aware of patterns and information in the family, develops hypotheses about what these patterns represent, and formulates relationship experiments and task assignments to test or alter the hypothesis on the basis of the information gathered (Figure 3-1). The therapist begins by making simple observations, then gradually makes hypotheses. When the therapist judges that a hypothesis is accepted, it can be used to construct an intervention and make a prediction about its outcome. If the prediction is accurate, the hypothesis is strengthened. In any case, new data that form the subject matter for further observation are generated. In one sense, the therapeutic cycle closes upon itself; in another, it develops spirally as the hypotheses become more and more refined. The therapist continues to learn from an interview; the hypothesis-testing model is a learning model. Although a therapist may be *implicitly* aware of these processes, the model makes the therapist *explicitly* aware of them. A clinical case may serve to clarify application of this model to the triangular processes operating in a child-centered family.

Chris is an 11-year-old with peer problems; he has few friends, is picked on by older children, and spends time with younger ones. Mostly, he is isolated or spends time with adults. He and his mother, Jane, were seen for 1½ years in individual therapy at a local child guidance clinic. His father, Adrian, was not involved.

Figure 3-1 Hypothesis-Testing Model

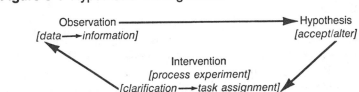

Observation ————————————→ Hypothesis
[data——→information]   *[accept/alter]*

Intervention
[process experiment]
[clarification——→task assignment]

Chris has had a history of school-related problems beginning with the transition to school during which he was described by his mother as "psychosomatic" and "schoolphobic." This was further complicated by Chris' special needs as a young child; he had previously been physically confined because of a hip deformity. Historically, Jane has been very involved with Chris and his school problems, as well as being primary caregiver when he was in braces to correct his physical handicap. His father has historically been in the distant position.

A series of nodal events coincided to create sufficient stress to activate the triangulation process in several interlocking triangles that have continued to be relatively fixed for the last 12 years. During Chris' first year of life, Jane's father died. Jane and 10-month-old Chris remained in England, while Adrian relocated in the United States, making provisions for his family to join him 6 months later.

The interlocking primary parental and intergenerational triangles were triggered again when Chris was 6 years old. Again, the developmental transition of Chris beginning school coincided with Jane's concern about her mother's health. Chris, being sensitized to his mother's upset regarding her extended family, became symptomatic. This also coincided with the covert marital conflict surfacing on the issues of sharing parental responsibility. This pattern has continued to recycle and remains the context for the presenting problem.

The hypothesis-testing model can be applied to the relevant triangles in this child-centered family with a school-related problem: the primary parental triangle, the auxiliary intergenerational triangles, and the triangles in the school context.

The Primary Parental Triangle

The therapist makes observations (gathers data) that form the basis of hypotheses about the flow of movement in the primary parental triangle of the family (Figure 3-2). Initial interventions either confirm or alter the original hypothesis. Once the hypothesis is confirmed, initial structural interventions are prescribed as tasks.

In the case example, the hypothesis is that Chris is triangled into the primary parental triangle by his sensitization to his mother's anxiety; his father is in the distant position. The process in the primary parental triangle is that the mother shows a great deal of anxiety; the father is at a distance from her; and the child, sensitized to his mother's anxiety, converts that anxiety into his school problem and his isolation. At any given time, the configuration of the triangle may be (1) mother and son overclose with

Figure 3-2 Hypothesis-Testing Model and the Primary Parental Triangle

Observation (data)	Hypothesis (accept/alter)
1. Mother, son sitting close together; father sitting across the room	1. Father distant
2. Comparison of amount of mother-son time versus father-son time at home	2. Mother and son overclose

Intervention
(structural)

Reverse flow of movement in triangle; build father-son relationship, and decrease mother's overinvolvement

---

father in the distant position or (2) mother and father close with problem son in the outside position.

The observation in the session shows the mother and son are sitting close to each other while the father is on the other side of the room. The description of the amount of relationship time and the character of their connectedness supports the hypothesis that mother and son are overclose and that father is in the outside position.

The relationship experiments (interventions) designed to reverse the flow of movement in this primary parental triangle form the first part of the overall treatment plan. These tasks are to move father and son closer together, and to move mother out to give father and son more time and space to work out a relationship. In the following dialogue, Guerin's beginning interventions to test the viability of the father-son relationship can be seen. He gathers information to build a bridge between Chris and his father to begin to close the distance, which increases the stress in the family. Chris triangles in to block Guerin's move, with the question "How old is my mother?" The sequence escalates with Chris writing his mother's age on the genogram. Guerin counters this by paying attention to Chris, initially engaging him in a light repartee, then returning to the issue at hand, the over-distant father-son relationship.

> Guerin: Do you ever spend any time sharing with your father some 11-year-old wisdom to help him out with his day, y'know?
>
> Chris: (*laughs*) No.
>
> Guerin: No?

Chris: He usually shares wisdom with me.

Guerin: He shares his 37-year-old wisdom with you?

Chris: How old is my mother?

Guerin: How old is your mother? They didn't put that up there. She made [your therapist] promise not to put it up there.

Chris.   (*to mother*) How old are you?

Guerin: (*laughs*) She's not going to tell you. What did I ask you before you interrupted? Did you forget? You're mad because your mother isn't going to tell you how old she is, right? We're going to have to replay the videotape to find out what I asked you. What did I ask you?

Chris: I don't know.

Adrian: You were discussing his . . . school. He mentioned that she dropped it.

Guerin: Well, I was thinking about something, but I forgot now.

Guerin continues to focus on the distant father-son relationship; he is looking for a bridge, an area of shared interest, to lay the groundwork to coach Adrian on ways to build a one-to-one relationship with his son. Guerin makes direct and indirect interventions to find a connection between the father and son. His strategies include negotiation.

Guerin: What would you like to do with your father, you know, I mean if you were picking it. Do you think his spending more time with you is a burden for him, or do you think he really wants to?

Chris: I think he'd more or less like to do electronics work and work on the car.

Guerin: Are you interested in that?

Chris: No. I'm more interested in doing father-son things like Playland, going skiing, stuff like that.

Guerin: Yeah.

Chris: And he says it's time-consuming and all that stuff, and so we don't go.

Guerin: You don't have any interest in cars and electronics and all that stuff. Do you think if you got more interested in that your father would get more interested in Playland?

(*systematizing the problem without taking sides*)

Guerin: He's a teacher, y'know, he could teach you a lot.

Chris: I don't know. When I grow up, I'm going to be a scientist or a psychologist, one of the two.

Guerin: I see. Well, y'know the stuff your father does has a connection to science. . . . You're not so sure.

Chris: More or less a psychologist, I'd like to be.

Guerin: Did he teach you about how a car works? . . .

Chris: I know more or less the basics because I watch him work. He tells me what he does.

Guerin: Does he let you hold the flashlight?

Chris: Yeah, that's basically what I do get to do, hold the flashlight.

Guerin: A "go-fer" and a holder. Do you like that?

Chris: No, but I do it to help.

Guerin: Does he let you put a few screws in every once in awhile? Do you like that?

Chris: Yeah.

Guerin: But you're not enthusiastic about it. So you two guys have a problem because you're not enthusiastic about what your dad's really enthusiastic about, and he's not awful enthusiastic about what you're enthusiastic about.

(*and a reversal*)

Guerin: Maybe you and your father are misfits, you know, as a father and son; you like different things, and you're both kind of loners. Getting you together is going to be a big problem.

The essence of a reversal is humor; it is the nature of a reversal to appear outrageous. Weary after fruitless attempts to counter emotional overinvolvement with rational persuasion, the therapist concocts an entertainment in which the individual's premises are reinforced to the point of absurdity and beyond. The best reversals promote a sudden backlash response from the patient. Guerin uses the reversal here to "twit" the father and son, rather than pushing them directly. Instead of trying to resolve their differences, he amplifies them, saying that the father and son are not likely to become close. Then, he normalizes the distant relationship ("It's something that goes on all over the world.") and anticipates the "recoil."

The First Intergenerational Triangle

In addition to the primary parent triangle, there are several interlocking auxiliary triangles that must be considered. The first of the auxiliary triangles to be applied to Chris and his family is the intergenerational triangle that includes the symptomatic child, a parent, and a grandparent. A child may get caught in the process of such a three-generational triangle because of the emotional process that is triggered by a significant death, most often that of a grandparent. The anxiety and upset surrounding such a loss may be bound into the relationship between a parent and a child, particularly a child who is born in the period approximately 2 years before or after the grandparent's death. Furthermore, this child may in later years appear to be sensitized to periods of increased anxiety and emotional upheaval on that side of the extended family.

In tracking the onset of a problem in its intergenerational context, hypotheses are derived by tracking those transitions that coincided with periods during which the problem recurred (Figure 3-3). Often, these events reinforce each other to form a "cluster stress" in which the problem is embedded; family members may confirm that they themselves felt a shift in the family climate. The organizational structure of the family may shift, then continue in the same pattern. Each member's options are narrowed, and there is limited movement.

At this point, the therapist transforms the genogram data into usable information by tracking the cluster stress. In Chris' family, there is evidence to support the hypothesis that Chris is caught in the three-generational triangle with his mother and grandmother. There was a shift in the family system in response to the stress associated with the death of Jane's father. At that time, Adrian moved to the United States, and Jane took Chris, who was then 10 months old, to help care for her mother following her father's death.

The interlocking of the two triangles—primary parent and intergenerational—was fixed at that time with Adrian in the distant position and Jane in a care-giving, overclose relationship with her son and her mother. Guerin explores the hypothesis that this intergenerational triangle continues to be

---

Figure 3-3 Hypothesis-Testing Model and the Intergenerational Triangle

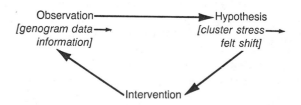

fixed. He questions whether Jane remains involved in the role of her
mother's caregiver by tracking

1. the extent to which the death of Jane's father is a taboo topic
2. the health of Jane's mother and Chris' reactions to Jane's upset
3. Jane's present involvement with her mother.

There is evidence the death of Jane's father, while not a taboo topic, is a
sensitive one that is not freely discussed.

Guerin: How upset do you remember being during the time of
your dad's death and Adrian coming over here? And
essentially what you had was your dad died and then
moving back in with a very upset mother and your
husband taking off for the States to set up his new work
thing. So was that an upsetting time for you?

Jane: I think it was very upsetting when my father died. I don't
think I really got over that when Adrian left. Because
even then that was difficult for me to even mention his
name or really, it was funny to think about him without
becoming upset.

Guerin: How about now, how do you do?

Jane: Well, the funny thing is now I'm talking more about him, I
feel myself becoming upset.

Guerin: Like, right this minute, you mean? Is that an experience
for you that's gone on over . . . he's been dead 11, 12
years.

Jane: Not really; at certain times. Not very often as a matter of
fact.

Guerin: Do you on purpose talk about him with your mother,
your brother, Adrian?

Jane: Not on purpose, but he will come up maybe in conversation.

Guerin: So you really had an awful lot to deal with while you
were trying to deal with your first year of mothering, too.
It was during Chris' first year, his first 2 years of life your
dad died, your family kind of got separated off.

Jane: I wouldn't say I had a lot of worry as such. I mean, there
was a lot of sadness there.

Guerin: Yeah, emotional upheaval or something.

Jane: Yes, yes.

Guerin: Was mothering easy for you?

Jane: Oh, yes.

Guerin: So it was kind of an easy thing for you.

Jane: Oh, yes, to mother Chris was very easy, I enjoyed that. In fact, it may be even having Chris helped me get over losing my father I suppose. I never thought about [it] but it does make sense to me.

Interventions for reversing the flow of movement in this intergenerational triangle include coaching Jane to reconnect with her family of origin, particularly around issues of unresolved grief about her father.

The Second Intergenerational Triangle

The second intergenerational triangle apparent in this family is the four-generational pattern of distance between father and son. Chris is triangled into a series of interlocking triangles in his father's family of origin (Figure 3-4). Adrian and his mother similarly had a special relationship with his father in a distant position. Going back another generation, Adrian's father never lived with his natural father, but was placed in a foster home. The pattern of distance between father and son over several generations is striking. In the following dialogue, Guerin asks Adrian for his thoughts on this pattern between him and his own father, between his father and grandfather, and between himself and Chris. Guerin attempts to encourage Adrian to develop a relationship with his own father to reverse this pattern.

Guerin: Do you think you and Chris are going to make it? So many fathers and their sons never make it. Did you make it with your father?

Figure 3-4 Intergenerational Pattern of Father-Son Distance

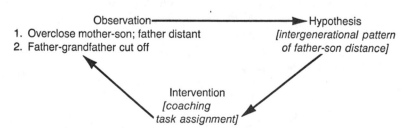

Observation ——————————————▶ Hypothesis
1. Overclose mother-son; father distant   *[intergenerational pattern*
2. Father-grandfather cut off   *of father-son distance]*

Intervention
*[coaching
task assignment]*

Adrian: When you say make it . . . do you mean work it out, really close?
Guerin: I mean having a solid relationship.
Adrian: I didn't work it out with my father, it's true.
Guerin: So you're one of the ones that didn't work it out with your dad. I mean there's millions of 'em out there. Fathers and sons seem to have huge problems connecting with one another. Do you think you and Chris are going to make it?
Adrian: Well, with the odds you've just put across, it doesn't look as if it might be that way.
Guerin: Are you hopeless about it?
Adrian: No, not at all. Despondent, no.
Guerin: So, you're going to make an effort still, even though the odds are against you.
Guerin: Was there ever a thing wherein your closeness to your mother was an issue for you and your father?
Adrian: Not a major issue.
Guerin: At least it wasn't up on the surface.
Adrian: That's right. Behind the scenes that may have taken place. . . . I can say my mother came to my defense constantly and that, of course, would go against the grain as far as my father would view it.
Guerin: So, that lined the two of you up with him on the outside.
Chris: Sounds like me.

Guerin lays the groundwork for Adrian's relationship experiment: to begin work on developing a one-to-one personal relationship with his father. He "coaches" Adrian on ways to reconnect with his father by encouraging Adrian to

1. make predictions about his father's reaction and plan ways to lighten the atmosphere. As Adrian predicts that his father would be "baffled," Guerin comments, "Is it nice to baffle a 60-year-old man?" and "If you started asking questions like that . . . he'd think the American air got you daft!"
2. contract for continued coaching with the therapist.
3. write a letter directly to his father telling him of the "project" he has begun (connecting with Chris), asking him for advice, and discovering more about his father's relationship with his own father.

Guerin: I just wondered. Would you be bitter about your experi-
          ence with him?
Adrian: Yes, if you're looking at bitter or not bitter, I'd say bitter,
          yes.
Guerin: Would it be entrenched enough bitterness to keep you
          from making an effort to connect with him at this point?
Adrian: No, as I say I feel I have an open mind on that.
Guerin: So, you'd be willing to entertain it as a possibility.

The School Context

In the child-centered family with a school-related problem, it is most important to look at the interlocking triangles embedded in the context of the school system and how it interfaces with the family system. The first of these triangles is the one in which the child's vulnerability in the family system does not show up explicitly within the family, but is played out in the child's peer network. Chris, like his father, sees himself as the rational problem solver; vis-à-vis his peers, he is in a distant, isolated position.

Chris: Well, if somebody is teasing me and I'm real upset, I'll
          keep to myself and then say, like someone is hurting
          another kid, I'll step in and say, why are you doing it?
          And if they were to, oh, they hit me in the head with a
          snowball, then I'd think why'd he do it and I'd ask him
          why.
Guerin: So, when you're upset, you like to be by yourself, and
          you are kind of a reasonable person, and you like things
          to work smoothly. In those ways, you'd be like your dad.

The hypothesis of a covert alliance between father and son would lead to interventions in which the therapist coaches Adrian to build a more explicit relationship with his son.

The second relevant triangle involves the symptomatic child caught in a conflict with a teacher or other authority figure as a result of an underlying conflict between the parents and/or stress in the extended family. The conflict may be implicit or explicit. In the case of Chris, the conflict is implicit and initially took the form of refusal to attend school. At the onset of this symptom, multiple factors combined to form a sufficiently stressful context: the intergenerational triangle in which Chris, sensitized as an infant to stress in his mother's family, is triangled with his mother and her concerns about her mother's health, and the surfacing of marital conflict around parenting issues. In the following dialogue, Jane outlines some of the problems between her and Adrian at the onset of Chris' symptoms.

> Jane: ... there were problems between Adrian and I inasmuch as Adrian wouldn't help me with Chris and the braces. He was forever saying you can do this, you can do that, but I didn't get any type of help from him. And Chris was a heavy boy to carry about.
>
> Guerin: So, that was kind of a perennial problem and the thing of Adrian expecting from you that you would handle all of that.
>
> Jane: Yes. I didn't mind handling certain things so much because I knew Adrian was pressured anyway. I think it was more our relationship that bothered me. I didn't think we were as close as what we should be. There was a lot of things missing.

Jane's reactivity to Adrian led to yet another triangle, one in which her conflict with the school administration was based in part on Adrian's profession—a schoolteacher. In this context, she increased her focus on Chris, putting more pressure on him and on the school to get more services and to arrange for a transfer to another school.

Interventions focus on relevant issues in the marital conflict. In this family, they involve dissecting the pursuit-distance pattern in the marriage, assigning tasks to modify this pattern, and placing it in an intergenerational context.

CONCLUSION

With the structural alterations in the primary parent triangle, the father's increased involvement with Chris, and the improvement in the father-son relationship, Chris' school behavior problem decreased considerably. There was a marked decrease in his isolation, an improvement in his adjustment at school, and an increase in his play network outside school. Jane began to show signs of a mild-to-moderate depressive reaction, although on an intellectual level she had accomplished her stated goal of bringing together her son and his father. The shift in the triangle put her on the outside and produced her symptoms, which were then linked to unresolved grief and mourning processes resulting from the death of her father and from her worries about her mother's declining health. Focus on these issues, using the interventions of coaching and letter writing, alleviated some of this distress. Intimacy in the couple was somewhat improved. Therapy was interrupted when Adrian was offered an excellent job in England and the family re-emigrated.

REFERENCES

Bowen, M. *Family therapy in clinical practice*. New York: Jason Aronson, 1966.

Ferber, A., Mendelsohn, M., and Napier, A. (Eds.). *The book of family therapy*. New York: Science House, 1972.

Fogarty, T. Triangles. *The Family*, 1975, 2(2), 41–49.

Guerin, P.J., & Gordon, E. Trees, triangles and temperament in the child-centered family. In C. Fishman & B. Rossman (Eds.), *Models for family change*. New York: Guilford Press, 1984.

Guerin, P.J., & Guerin, K.B. Theoretical aspects and clinical relevance of the multi-generational model of family therapy. In P.J. Guerin (Ed.), *Family therapy: Theory and practice*. New York: Gardner Press, 1976.

Guerin, P.J., & Pendagast, E.G. Evaluation of family system and genogram. In P.J. Guerin (Ed.), *Family therapy: Theory and practice*. New York: Gardner Press, 1976.

Katz, A. *Intimacy: The role of awareness in young adult couples*. Unpublished doctoral dissertation, Boston University, 1978.

Katz, A. *Family therapy training program curriculum*. Lexington, MA: Mystic Valley Mental Health Center, 1981.

Minuchin, S. *Families and family therapy*. Cambridge, MA: Harvard University Press, 1974.

Pendagast, E.G., & Sherman, C.O. A guide to the genogram. In *The best of the family 1973–1978*. New Rochelle, NY: Center for Family Learning, 1979.

Satir, V. *Conjoint family therapy*. Palo Alto, CA: Science & Behavior Books, 1967.

4. Therapy with a Family with a Learning-Disabled Child

Celia Spacone
James C. Hansen, PhD
State University of New York at Buffalo

THE LEARNING-DISABLED CHILD IS AN ENIGMA FOR EDUCATORS, MENTAL health professionals, and the medical community. Because the etiology, definition, and treatment are not mutually agreed upon by the various professionals who come in contact with such children, the group that bears the label *learning-disabled* is large and diverse. The recent trend to recognize the behavioral and emotional impacts of the disability has added a new dimension to the puzzle.

Family therapists have become involved with these children as the interaction between the learning disability and the family system has been recognized. The family may be stressed by the presence of a learning-disabled child and the resulting need to keep boundaries flexible and accept the variety of community agencies that become involved. Furthermore, patterns in the family may maintain and exacerbate the disability. Family therapists need to be prepared to work with such families.

EMOTIONAL CHARACTERISTICS OF THE LEARNING-DISABLED CHILD

Coming to a consensus about what constitutes a learning disability has been a consistent problem in this field. In 1981, six professional organizations sent representatives to a national joint committee for learning disabilities and arrived at the following definition:

Learning Disabilities is a generic term that refers to a hetero-geneous group of disorders manifested by significant difficulties in the acquisition and use of listening, speaking, reading, writing, reasoning, or mathematical abilities. These disorders are intrinsic to the individual and presumed to be due to central nervous system dysfunction. Even though a learning disability may occur concomitantly with other handicapping conditions (e.g., sensory impairment, mental retardation, social and emotional disturbances) or environmental influences (e.g., cultural differences, insufficient/inappropriate instruction, psychogenic factors), it is not the direct result of those conditions or influences. (Hammill, Leigh, McNutt, & Larsen, 1981, p. 336)

The impact of such attempts at definition is not clear. Kirk and Kirk (1983) commented that the general consensus is that few practitioners pay any attention to the numerous definitions. While 76% of the 149 professionals in the field of learning disabilities who were questioned by Tucker, Stevens, and Ysseldyke (1983) replied that learning disabilities are clinically identifiable by symptoms different from the effects of varying cultural or educational opportunities, there was wide disagreement on the incidence rate. This suggests a disparity in diagnosis. Professionals may feel they operate from clear, differential criteria; nationwide, however, there is little consensus on the characteristics of the learning-disabled population. Cases must be reviewed on an individual basis.

The syndrome does have some commonly recognized characteristics. Anxiety is identified as an almost universal problem with the learning-disabled child (Solan, 1981). It may be difficult to discern whether the anxiety and hyperactivity that often accompany a learning disability are primary or secondary to the disability. Poor concentration, short attention span, distractibility, aggressive behavior, and depression are concomitant symptoms.

Solan (1981) identified three adaptive reactions that are often seen in the learning-disabled child: withdrawal, regression, and clowning. The learning-disabled child who withdraws becomes passive and may revert to inner fantasy to avoid the anxiety of failure. A child who displays a regressive reaction reverts to an earlier stage of social, emotional, or intellectual development that demands less of the child. Solan identified the clowning reaction as the most serious, for it often results in asocial behavior and trouble with the school; the child takes the stance that he or she does not learn solely because of a personal choice not to learn.

The withdrawal reaction occurs most frequently in rigid, conflict-avoiding families in which family secrets abound. The regressive reaction is seen when at least one of the parents is overprotective and enmeshed with the child. The clowning reaction is more apparent when parental disagreements over achievement are unresolved or when the child experiences a disengaged system. Usually, there is a triangle in operation, and the problem behavior is quietly endorsed by one of the parents.

In his discussion of the characteristics of the "truly brain damaged child," that is, the child who exhibits the so-called hard neurological signs, Christ (1978) presented a framework for dealing with these cognitive and emotional factors in psychotherapy. Although he wrote from an individual perspective, his notions can be helpful in a more systemically oriented approach. Christ contended that a crucial determination to be made is the stage of cognitive organization (Piaget, 1952) that the child has attained. A child who is only at the preoperational stage (unlike a child at the concrete and formal operational stages), regardless of chronological or mental age, does not identify another person's world view. This child cannot imagine how another person may think or feel, see the subtleties of situations, or make decisions by weighing various circumstances. A child at this stage does not possess the repertoire of concrete operational strategies:

> Concrete operational strategies include the ability to conserve—to see that things and situations have more than one dimension—and to decenter—to put oneself in another's place or to understand that a sequence of events can be seen from more than one perspective. (Christ, 1978, p. 508)

Nor does such a child possess the formal operational cognitive strategies:

> Formal operational cognitive strategies include the ability to start with all hypothetical possibilities and deduct concrete examples from the possible, as well as the ability to think about the relationship of ideas to ideas. (Christ, 1978, p. 508)

Thus, if another child makes a sharp remark to a child in the preoperational stage, he or she does not wonder about the variety of causal factors (e.g., the other child was in a bad mood or was envious) that may have been in operation, but instead tends to react in a black and white, all or none fashion.

Change of any type is particularly threatening for these children, for they cannot project into the future and see that homeostasis will return. Children at the preoperational stage are not appropriate candidates for insight-oriented psychotherapy. In family therapy, interventions that directly involve this type of child are most appropriately structural in nature. In addition, Christ contended that, because most learning-disabled youngsters rely primarily on denial or projection as defense mechanisms, they must develop a store of more usable or "negotiable" defense mechanisms. Such a store enables these children to participate more freely in discussions of their problems and to participate in insight-oriented psychotherapy.

THE FAMILY OF THE LEARNING-DISABLED CHILD

Most studies on the families of learning-disabled children have centered on the mother-child dyad and its role in perpetuating the learning difficulty. Staver (1953), for example, used a case study approach to investigate 17 families, each having a child (6 to 13 years of age) with a learning problem that left the child at least 1 year behind in school achievement. Focusing on the mothers, Staver found that they seemed preoccupied with fears of separation and/or illness in this child. At the time of the learning-disabled child's birth, there had been a traumatic event or threat of one that implied separation or loss. Staver's observation was that "mother and child cling to each other with an attachment which leaves them unclearly differentiated as separate persons" (p. 134).

Humphries and Bauman (1980) compared the responses of mothers of normal achievers with the responses of mothers of learning-disabled children on the Parent Attitude Research Instrument. The mothers of the learning-disabled scored significantly higher on the authoritarian and control (strict, restrictive, suppressive attitude) factor, but these same mothers also reported less hostility and rejection toward their children. The authors noted that these findings could suggest a trend toward "excessive dependency" by the learning-disabled children.

One of the first significant investigations beyond the mother-child dyad was made by Grunebaum, Hurwitz, Prentice, and Sperry (1962) in their clinical study of the fathers of sons with a primary neurotic learning disability. They noted that, even though many of the fathers had attained some level of educational and occupational success, they were still self-derogatory and unsatisfied, described themselves as feeling thwarted from their "ideal" goals, and attributed their success to "luck." Those fathers who were not successful accepted their status with a sense of hopeless resignation. Although the mothers of these learning-disabled sons were not the primary area of the investigation, Grunebaum and colleagues noted that the mother generally concurred with the father's self-image and extended the sense of failure about the husband to the family system: "The mother . . . considers her husband an inadequate man and subtly limits and devalues him in relation to his executive function in the home, specifically with the children" (p. 465). The father's role in the home was passive, marked by occasional outbursts of violent or uncontrolled anger that strengthened the mother's notion of the father as an ineffective parent. In abandoning that parental role, the father acted as the son's rival for the love and attention of the mother.

Gradually, investigators have begun to expand their focus to consider the family as a whole rather than as a group of individual dyads. In 1955, Fabian studied reading-disabled populations in a variety of settings and concluded that familial psychopathology had to be considered one of several causal factors. This is certainly a cognitive leap on Fabian's part, particularly for the vast majority of cases, but later investigators have in fact found several social and emotional factors that are associated with poor achievement and can be linked to familial traits.

Kohn and Rosman (1974) used hierarchical regression techniques and determined that measures of the social and emotional factors of apathy, withdrawal, and task orientation provided the most information in predicting early elementary school achievement. They were further able to link these findings to family investigations. Children who showed a great deal of apathy and withdrawal had controlling parents and were made fearful of the environment; those with low scores on task orientation were likely to have experienced rejection, neglect, and a disorganized family life. Thus, these findings offer some support for the notion that certain familial traits are associated with poor academic achievement.

The kinetic family drawings of 50 perceptually delayed kindergarten children were analyzed by Raskin and Pitcher-Baker (1977). They found that the perceptually delayed group displayed significantly more indicators of isolation-rejection, body concerns, and sibling rivalry on their family drawings.

According to family systems theory, symptom maintenance can serve a function in a family system in which the disability is promoted or provoked. Although they did not write from a systems perspective, Silverman, Fite, and Mosher (1959) shed some light on this issue through their observations. They summarized data from 35 case studies of reading-disabled children (predominantly latency-aged boys) and arrived at a profile of a typical reading-disabled child. They noticed what they considered atypical patterns in the families of the children studied, patterns that they felt somehow related to the disability:

> Frequently, there would be only one parent actively concerned or present in such a child's family. In addition, this child would manifest severe rivalry with siblings. . . . The parents themselves, of such a child, would often be found to have suffered from a disturbed traumatic childhood, and frequently have histories of mental illness or breakdown. They would probably be involved in serious marital discord. One or both parents, moreover, would have undesirable attitudes regarding academic achievement and apply undue pressure on the child, perhaps because they themselves had had learning difficulties. The data showed that there was a surprisingly high incidence of school failure and learning disability on the part of parents and siblings of the typical child. (p. 306)

If these findings are interpreted in a systems perspective, it might be inferred that the family may maintain or reinforce the disability to defer attention from marital discord or unmet parental desires for achievement.

Case analyses of 18 boys from an outpatient psychiatric hospital support this notion (Miller & Westman, 1964). The boys were between 10 and 12 years of age, had an average IQ, were at least 2 years retarded in reading, and had not responded to intensive remedial help. Miller and Westman postulated that the reading disability was being used to ensure the family's survival. Their cases showed four trends as evidence of this notion:

1. The child's symptom and subidentity were often compatible with those of the parents (i.e., lack of achievement and questions of competence in the parents).
2. Many family members engaged in activities that reinforced the symptom in the child.
3. Members of the family reacted emotionally to improved reading as if it were a major emergency.
4. Adults denied solid evidence of the child's unmet potential. The notion that parents of the learning-disabled tend to underestimate the child's potential has received much support in the literature (Foster & Lomas, 1978; Epstein, Berg-Cross, & Berg-Cross, 1980; Klein, Allman, Dreizen, Friedman, & Powers, 1981; Parkinson, Wallis, Prince, & Harvey, 1982).

Kaslow and Cooper (1978), who are family therapists, have characterized the reactions of parents as they first confront the reality of having a less than perfect child as parallel to a grief and mourning process. First there is denial, then depression, anger, and finally guilt over the thought that they may have been responsible in some way for their child's handicap. Later, parents often compensate by becoming overprotective and overindulgent, which effectively deprives the child of further opportunities for growth and development. The child often becomes skilled at manipulating the parents and can assume the role of a central, powerful, and subtly controlling member of the family.

Over time, because the parents of a learning-disabled child invest a great deal of energy in that child, they may become tired, anxious, and angry. Kaslow and Cooper (1978) suggested that one of four maladaptive relationship patterns may emerge, affecting the child's emotional and intellectual progress. The parents may become irritable, and the marital relationship may be marred by arguments and reproachments. Second, one parent, most often the mother, may become quite depressed, and this emotion may hover around her and the child. Third, one spouse may see himself or herself as the child's protector and form an enmeshed alliance with the child against the other parent. This shuts out the other parent, who may turn to work, leisure activities, or an extramarital affair to offset the disappointment and loneliness. The enmeshed parent then assumes a stance of self-sacrifice and devotion to the child. Finally, both parents may compete for the child's attention and affection.

In a report of their clinical observations, Day and Moore (1976) listed 10 patterns they often find in families with a learning-disabled child:

1. inhibition of aggressiveness and competitiveness
2. hostile dependency and fear of growth
3. passive-aggressive retaliation, intense but often covert power
4. negative self-image, depression, self-depreciation, and self-punishment
5. guilt in the parent or the child that inhibits aggression and opposition
6. inhibition of conflict because of the fear of provoking rejection
7. infantilization or overprotection of a child because of parental insecurity
8. family scapegoating
9. parental projections that are acted out by the child
10. maintaining "family secrets"

In summary, when the family reacts maladaptively to a learning disability, several patterns appear to be prevalent. Overprotection and control on the part of at least one parent, most often the mother, seems to be a consistent finding. The second parent, most often the father, appears distant and "left out" of the family. The family may be enmeshed and rigid, avoiding conflict and its resolution by deferring attention to the child. This combination of patterns appears similar to Minuchin's (1974) model of the psychosomatic family in which the child is physiologically vulnerable and the family is characterized by enmeshment, overprotectiveness, rigidity, and lack of conflict resolution. Minuchin, Rossman, and Baker (1978) also suggested that the child's problem reinforces the family's pattern of avoiding conflict, which in turn reinforces the symptoms. The typical patterns of child involvement are triangulation, parent-child coalition, and detouring.

It has been speculated that a parallel process occurs with learning disabilities (Perosa, 1980). There may be a primary neurological dysfunction that is then exacerbated in some cases by enmeshed, overprotective, rigid families that avoid conflict by detouring and triangulation. When Perosa compared the interactions of families with a learning-disabled child with the interactions of a norm group of families, families with a learning-disabled child were found to function more as psychosomatic families do than as average families do. However, she found some differences between psychosomatic families and families with a learning-disabled child. The latter displayed some neglect rather than overprotection and some disengagement rather than enmeshment. When neglect and disengagement occurred, they were evidenced in the fathers of the learning-disabled children. Thus, the implication for the learning-disabled child is an enmeshed, overprotective mother and a disengaged, distant father.

THERAPEUTIC INTERVENTION

The Smiths are a white, middle-class family. Mr. Smith (40 years of age) was employed in a white collar position, and Mrs. Smith (39 years of age) was a homemaker. They had been married 16 years and had three children. Ron, the eldest, was 14, was considered to be a model student, and was very active in sports and social activities. The youngest child, Roger, was 8 and was achieving well at school, but he was rather socially immature.

Tom (12 years of age) was the identified client. The family was referred by the school because of Tom's disruptive behavior in his class. Tom's development had appeared to be normal until the age of 4, when he suffered a severe trauma to the left hemisphere of his brain as a result of a fall down the basement stairs to the cement floor below. Tom's injury resulted in a temporary (1 week) loss of speech functioning. Frequent hospitalizations were required for 1 year after the accident to replace a section of his fractured skull. Tom experienced occasional epileptic seizures and hyperactive symptoms for 3 to 4 years after the injury. At the time of referral, medication was effectively controlling the epilepsy, and the hyperactive symptoms had ceased. Tom had spent his entire academic career in classes for the learning-disabled. He was experiencing difficulty even in keeping up with the adjusted curriculum. His peer and teacher relationships were very poor and were marked by inadequate impulse control on Tom's part. He teased other children unmercifully, particularly when he was in a group situation. In the classroom, his interactions with the teachers were acceptable only if he had the teacher's complete attention or he was involved in a highly structured activity.

The home situation was marked by much fighting among the Smith children, most of it between Tom and his younger brother, Roger. The parents, particularly Mrs. Smith, often intervened to stop the fights, which were felt to be provoked by Tom. Tom was most often disciplined by being sent to his room, where he would destroy his own belongings in a fit of rage. In fact, Tom often chose to withdraw to his room and spent many hours there alone.

In the course of therapy, a variety of techniques were employed, all within the organizational framework of Minuchin's structural family therapy. In this model, a therapeutic plan was established to change the family so that its structure would become more consistent with the model of a normal family at a given stage in its development, with appropriate consideration of its cultural and socioeconomic context. Some individual and subsystem boundaries may need to be established, differentiating enmeshed members and increasing the involvement of disengaged members. The therapist begins by joining and accommodating to the system, but retains enough independence to resist the family's pull and to challenge the family at various times. Therefore, the therapist becomes a boundary maker, intensifier, and general change agent in the session.

It became apparent that Mrs. Smith and her children, but most blatantly Tom, were highly enmeshed. At times, a coalition of secrecy developed between Mrs. Smith and Tom to "protect" father from hearing about a bad day at school and becoming upset. Mr. Smith had cut himself off from the family and had retreated into his work. Mrs. Smith's overinvolvement and overprotection of Tom had left her husband resentful and angry. Furthermore, there was a family ban on conflict expression. Mr. Smith said he could not discipline Tom because he was afraid of becoming "too angry" and losing control. Thus, he "ignored" Tom's behavior until he found it unbearable and then erupted in physical punishment. Mrs. Smith ineffectively tried to deal with Tom's misbehavior by herself. In conflicts with her husband, she tended to be in a low power position and responded by backing down rather than facing conflict.

A behavioral management program was instituted for home use. The parents were put in charge—as a team—of deciding whether to dispense rewards for Tom. As expected, this heightened marital conflict, which eventually erupted in a session. The interaction between parents was intensified by the therapists, who physically separated the parents from the sibling subsystem and then coached them to stay on the topic. With one of the therapists supporting her and offsetting the balance of power in the family, Mrs. Smith was able to work through and resolve several issues with her husband.

Various subsystems of the family were seen during the course of therapy. At times, the marital dyad worked on marital issues and ways to deal with Tom. One of the therapists also worked with Tom alone. It was decided that Tom was at a preoperational stage of development in which he was not able to see the world view of another. Stories, role plays, and TV programs were used as a basis for discussion on appreciating the other's world view. The parents were able to watch from a one-way mirror and observe the therapist working with Tom. Mr. Smith was put in charge of reading a story with Tom every night and discussing the character's feelings, motivations, and possible alternative methods of dealing with the dilemma in the story. This intervention was double-edged in that it was structurally aimed at strengthening the father-son dyad, while it also furthered Tom's cognitive and emotional development in the manner recommended previously by Christ (1978).

Tom's disability had been cloaked in an aura of secrecy that gradually dissipated in the family sessions. This was helpful for Tom in several ways. He began to see the link between his injury and his intellectual and emotional problems. His parents could openly discuss how Tom's need for structure and sameness resulted in his misbehavior when any change occurred in the family or at school. They were then able to anticipate and plan for such events.

It was felt that a key manifestation of the enmeshment between Mrs. Smith and Tom was the fact that they spent so much time together. For example, the school had responded to Tom's misbehavior by suspending him and having him stay home all day with his mother. When the therapists discussed the possibility of Tom's father taking a day off from work to stay home with Tom the next time he was suspended, Tom's suspension rate dropped to zero for the remainder of the school year.

Tasks and homework were often assigned to consolidate the changes that were made during the sessions and to extend these changes into the family's real world interactions. These tasks centered on involving Tom and his father in more positively focused direct interactions to defocus the mother-son alliance. The father-son reading task had this effect. When boundaries separating parental systems from those of the children are crossed inappropriately, triangles involving parents and child occur. Thus, tasks were given to restrengthen the boundary between the parents and the children. The parents were instructed to implement the behavior modification program as a team. Each night they conferred on whether Tom had earned extra time to stay up. Parents were encouraged to take a long-needed vacation together so that they could "recharge" to deal with the children better.

Changes were further effected in the sibling subsystem to decrease the negative interactions. The role of each sibling in the fights was identified after the brothers enacted their struggles while playing a game together. The three boys were then instructed to play a board game together where they earned points by acting in different ways. Ron, identified as a parental child, was instructed to stay out of all fights between Tom and Roger. Roger was seen as encouraging Tom's misbehavior by bursting into tears and whining at the smallest provocation. He was given points by the observer for behavior identified as "grown-up." Various behaviors that Tom needed to incorporate were also included in the weekly sessions (i.e., asking rather than demanding, acting like a big brother by teaching Roger how to play, using his voice in a nonabrasive fashion).

As a result of these therapeutic interventions, Tom's behavior improved so that he finished the school year without further incident. Misbehavior at home decreased, and Tom was able to participate in a sports activity during the summer. Tom's reactions were still rather impulsive, but parental acceptance of this was better; their reactions were more controlled and less punitive. A restructuring of the family had enabled them to function more appropriately. Although the structural model was the basic framework of therapy in this case, it is apparent that a variety of techniques are necessary with complex family problems involving learning disabilities.

REFERENCES

Christ, A.E. Psychotherapy of the child with true brain damage. *American Journal of Orthopsychiatry*, 1978, *48*(3), 505–515.

Day, J., & Moore, M. Individual and family psychodynamic contributions to learning disability. *Psychiatric Hospitals Journal*, 1976, *8*, 27–30.

Epstein, J., Berg-Cross, G., & Berg-Cross, L. Maternal expectations and birth order in families with learning disabled and normal children. *Journal of Learning Disabilities*, 1980, *13*(5), 45–52.

Fabian, A.A. Reading disability: An index of pathology. *American Journal of Orthopsychiatry*, 1955, *25*, 319–329.

Foster, R.M., & Lomas, D.F. Anger, disability and demands in the family. *American Journal of Orthopsychiatry*, 1978, *48*(2), 228–236.

Grunebaum, M.G., Hurwitz, I., Prentice, N.M., & Sperry, B.M. Fathers of sons with primary neurotic learning inhibitions. *American Journal of Orthopsychiatry*, 1962, *32*, 462–472.

Hammill, D.D., Leigh, J.E., McNutt, G., & Larsen, S.C. A new definition of learning disabilities. *Learning Disability Quarterly*, 1981, *4*(4), 336–342.

Humphries, T.W., & Bauman, E. Maternal child rearing attitudes associated with learning disabilities. *Journal of Learning Disabilities*, 1980, *13*(8), 54–57.

Kaslow, F., & Cooper, B. Family therapy with a learning disabled child and his/her family. *Journal of Marriage and Family Counseling*, 1978, *4*, 41–49.

Kirk, S.A., & Kirk, W.D. On defining learning disabilities. *Journal of Learning Disabilities*, 1983, *16*(1), 20–21.

Klein, R.S., Altman, S.D., Friedman, R., Dreiser, K., & Powers, L. Restructuring dysfunctional parental attitudes toward children's learning and behavior in school: Family-oriented psychoeducational therapy. Part II. *Journal of Learning Disabilities*, 1981, *14* (2), 99–101.

Kohn, M., & Rosman, B.L. Social-emotional, cognitive, and demographic determinants of poor school achievement: Implications for a strategy of interventions. *Journal of Educational Psychology*, 1974, *66*(2), 267–276.

Mahler-Schoenberger, M. Pseudo-imbecility: A magic cap of invisibility. *Psychoanalytic Quarterly*, 1942, *11*, 149–164.

Miller, D.R., & Westman, J.C. Reading disability as a condition of family stability. *Family Process*, 1964, *3*(1), 66–76.

Minuchin, S. *Families and family therapy*. Cambridge, MA: Harvard University Press, 1974.

Minuchin, S., Rossman, B., & Baker, L. *Psychosomatic families*. Cambridge, MA: Harvard University Press, 1978.

Parkinson, C.E., Wallis, S.M., Prince, J., & Harvey, D. Research note: Rating the home environment of school-age children. A comparison with general cognitive index and school progress. *Journal of Child Psychology and Psychiatry*, 1982, *23*(3), 329–333.

Perosa, L. The development of a questionnaire to measure Minuchin's structural family concepts and the application of his psychosomatic family model to learning disabled families. Dissertation, State University of New York at Buffalo, 1980.

Piaget, J. *The origins of intelligence in children*. New York: International Universities Press, 1952.

Raskin, L.M., & Pitcher-Baker, G. Kinetic family drawings by children with perceptual-motor delays. *Journal of Learning Disabilities*, 1977, *10*(6), 49–53.

Silverman, J.S., Fite, M.W., & Mosher, M.M. Clinical findings in reading disability children—Special cases of intellectual inhibition. *American Journal of Orthopsychiatry*, 1959, *29*(2), 298–314.

Solan, H.A. A rationale for the optometric treatment and management of children with learning disabilities. *Journal of Learning Disabilities*, 1981, *14*(10), 568–572.

Staver, N. The child's learning difficulty as related to the emotional problem of the mother. *American Journal of Orthopsychiatry*, 1953, *23*, 131–140.

Tucker, J., Stevens, L.J., & Ysseldyke, J.E. Learning disabilities: The experts speak out. *Journal of Learning Disabilities*, 1983, *16*(1), 6–19.

5. The Cycle of Poverty— Where To Begin?

David Kantor, PhD
Director, Kantor Family Institute
Cambridge, Massachusetts

Anne Peretz, MSW
Executive Director, The Family Center
Somerville, Massachusetts

Rosamund Zander, MSW
The Family Center
Somerville, Massachusetts

THE POOR ARE HERE, IN AMERICA, IN GREAT NUMBERS, AND THEY ARE here to stay. Within certain stable limits, their numbers inflate and deflate according to shifting political winds, which come and go in 4-year cycles. Carried along by these shifting winds, social programs that affect the lives of millions of poor are swept into and out of the existing institutional framework of human services unpredictably, or so it seems from the beneficiaries' point of view.

Public housing projects are an exception. Like the poor, they seem to be here to stay. Though nobly conceived as an efficient means of providing low-cost housing for the poor, they appear to have failed as a social experiment. The contagion effects of clustering poor with poor and problem with problem are at best difficult to contain. Thus, housing projects may create more problems than they cure; however, this does not stem the tides of the poor seeking entry.

It may not be the institutional form itself that has failed, but the programs of support and change that are designed by the helping industry and put in the service of the poor. Aside from the ways that the political economy and sociopolitical considerations bear on the problem, the issues are

1. Is family therapy, which now rests on a firm foundation as a treatment form after 30 years of groundwork, going to turn an elitist back on the poor as psychoanalytic psychiatry did, or will it apply its insights and techniques to what is admittedly a tremendously difficult problem from a humanistic as well as from a systems theory point of view?
2. Have our theoretical development and clinical know-how matured enough to continue the pioneering work carried out by the likes of Minuchin, Montalvo, and Auerswald in the early days of family therapy?
3. Will we devote ourselves to elegant but essentially insignificant solutions that give us a sense of professional satisfaction, but which address only a small manifestation of the problem, or will we devote ourselves to a search for interventions that count?

The criterion for "interventions that count" is singular, yet severe. It is summed up in the question: Do they interrupt the cycle of poverty that seeds many of the family problems that family therapists attempt to change? An interim question must also be posed, because the criterion cannot always be met when a therapy, even a "successful" one, is terminated: Are the interventions specifically designed to alter family structures that demonstrably maintain the cycle of poverty?

60

THE FAMILY CENTER PROGRAM

A program is being designed at The Family Center to serve families principally from the Cambridge-Somerville area of Massachusetts. Like other start-up programs, The Family Center has a mission, a self-conscious point of view. Because this program of therapy has not been separated from its context, it is systemic in principle, theory, and practice. It assumes that the problems manifested in these families are developmental crises, sometimes transient and temporary, sometimes enduring and chronic, and that it is important to make these distinctions.

The Family Center's program is structural. As in many other family therapy approaches, it is assumed that the first step in bringing about change in most instances is to identify the structure and process associated with the problem or symptom. Structure is considered a multilevel concept, however, and the level of structural intervention is of paramount importance if significant outcome, not just outcome, is to be achieved. For example, a school-resistant child's return to school might be a significant outcome in a middle-class family if the behavior reflects a triangle in which the teen-aged son is playing out his mother's hidden opposition to his father's pressure for achievement. It might not be a significant outcome in a disadvantaged poor family headed by an alcoholic mother if the truancy reflects a so-called disturbed hierarchy in which the teen-aged daughter's role is to rescue her mother and abused younger sister.

The focus in this program is on the interrelationship and reciprocal effects of four key elements:

1. the client
2. the therapist
3. the theoretical understanding of the disturbed structure
4. the technique chosen to address it

Thus, for example, therapists who are not sufficiently adaptable in their perceptions and vernacular to work convincingly with the disadvantaged poor do not do outreach work but are reserved for in-house work with more systemically intact families. Also, because disadvantaged poor families can wear down the therapists who seek to help them, the therapist's capacity to endure in outreach is taken into account and assignments varied to include both outreach and in-house work. Techniques such as brief strategic interventions are tactically employed in some cases to allow therapists who need relief to distance themselves; in other situations, however, techniques that allow more intimate engagement for therapists are devised. Clients representing a broad social spectrum are served in both outreach and in-house program activities.

Different client populations have distinctive characteristics that affect not only the level of structural intervention, but also techniques, therapist morale, and evaluation of outcome. A therapeutic program for disadvantaged poor families in public housing projects must be based on an understanding of the cycle of poverty and must derive its program emphases from a consideration of the particular, but now quite common, problems of these families, as well as the options therapists have for interventions.

THE CYCLE OF POVERTY

For the families in question, it all starts with poverty. A life of poverty reduces for the children of these families their chances for reasonably good health, educational achievement, and economic self-sufficiency. At risk in infancy, they are more likely to die in their first years of life than are other babies. At risk in young childhood, they are more likely to suffer from malnutrition, child abuse, and educational disability. At risk in adolescence, they are more likely to have problems such as alcohol and drug dependency, school resistance, delinquency, and teen-age pregnancy. With the onset of an unplanned pregnancy, the stage is set for the cycle to begin all over again. Actually, as Peacock (1981) pointed out, the cycle really began when the girls' mothers were adolescents themselves. She vividly described a ''perpetual cycle of women who become mothers without ever completing their own childhood'' (p. xiv). It seems that, if the cycle of poverty is to be broken, the key will come from an understanding of this mother-daughter-unplanned baby triad.

The histories of these families follow a relentlessly repetitive pattern: *poverty,* leading to *limitation of choice,* leading to *unplanned pregnancy,* leading to *protracted dependency,* leading to *poverty.* Early in the cycle, the unemployed or marginally employed fathers of the babies leave. Often, they are followed by other men who also impregnate the mothers and leave. The mothers, frequently only 14 to 16 years old at the time of their first unplanned pregnancy, are left without support and become dependent on welfare for economic support and on their own mothers for emotional support. ''Sometimes the babies are the only source of fulfillment these women have'' (Peacock, 1981, p. xiv). Given the job of raising children before they complete their own childhood, they simply lack the basic resources to do the job. Their mothers, who like them were developmentally derailed, serve more as friends and equals than as models for parenting, for dealing with men, or for developing survival skills as women. Because the girls were not adequately nurtured, disciplined, or prepared for real autonomy, they are incapable of instilling in their daughters a basic sense of trust, self-esteem, or competency—the requirements for reasonably healthy growth.

Mother-Daughter Dyad

Preparation of daughters for a close and too dependent tie with their mothers begins early in the cycle, with the phenomenon of the absent male. Because the mother-daughter dyad is the only hope for stable bonding, it plays an especially significant role in the cycle within the cycle of poverty. This one tells the story of mixed messages—"Go away and get out of my hair." and "Stay close and give me a baby that will keep us bonded."—a bind that bonds.

As pressing survival problems deplete the energies of these women, they require treatment for a string of physical and psychological maladies; many are given antidepressants for a condition not included in DMS III, a kind of psychic numbing that comes from sheer exhaustion and hopelessness. Because their lives are often disrupted by unpredictable emergencies, these women cannot put together for their children a coherent program for making it in the world. These children live, instead, under a social order in which rules invented for one moment are changed for the next, resulting in the nightmare consequences of a family system in runaway, rather than gradual, development. These mothers do not, and probably cannot, take the time to train children in the subtleties and nuances that distinguish "Do this because it is moral." from "Do this because I am desperate at this moment." As a result, there develops in these families what seems to be an arbitrary interchangeability between affectual and power exchanges that is very confusing to outsiders. To the mother and daughter, however, it is not confusing at all; it is only another step in getting on with the bind that bonds.

In the daughter's adolescence, the bind that bonds mother and daughter in a dubious dyadic alliance (and ultimately in a perverse triad, when the daughter gives birth), comes to life, literally and figuratively. Usually, the first payment on the debt that the daughter cannot escape at home is made in school. *School resistance* is the name given the first sign of trouble. The daughter becomes withdrawn in class, depressed, or unmotivated; she may develop school behavior problems, become truant, or exhibit schoolphobia.

Sometimes, daughters skip school simply to take care of mothers who are sick, alcoholic, depressed, or worn down and unable to care for other children.

Gradually, the girls leave school for the streets. Street life has a greater importance as a testing ground for adolescent autonomy, future identity, and a sense of competency even for those who remain in school than it has for children of more systemically advantaged, upwardly mobile, poor families or for children of middle-class families. In systemically disadvantaged families, children are not encouraged to achieve in school, to explore vocations, or to anticipate and avoid pitfalls, such as an unplanned pregnancy. It is street life that gives the girls whatever skills they are to attain. Along with the boys, they learn how to obtain beer and liquor illegally, deface property as a curbstone thrill, and defy police and other authorities. If the nonadaptive aspects of such skill mastery is an accident of social context, it is no less distressful. Ultimately, adolescence represents not the beginning, but the beginning of the end.

On the surface, the girls achieve a kind of independence, a temporary separation from family and from mother. Because they have not been adequately nurtured, however, their need to keep close to their mothers prevails. In spite of defiance, disobedience, outright rebellion, involvement in crimes, occasional running away, and a street toughness that reduces mothers' authority to a sham, they ultimately return home in search of the consistency of rules, the protection from the world and from their own uncultivated instincts, and, above all, the mothering that somehow escaped them. They do this through the "unplanned pregnancy."

Birth of a Baby

Once the baby is born, the mother, the daughter, and the baby are caught up in a web of enmeshing dependencies. Because the mother, too, never received the basic care and nurturing she needed, she covertly supports the entire circumstance, hoping somehow to redeem her own past and obtain what it failed to provide. Ambivalent though the daughter may be about having a baby, the opportunity to bring one home to her mother checks the guilt, anger, and unredeemed love that otherwise dominates the girl's feelings toward her mother.

The birth of a baby addresses another phenomenon for the young girl: as she has become familiar with the cycle in which her mother is caught up, the girl perceives few alternatives for herself. Chances are her mother sees herself only as a "mother." As this still growing child develops physically, her best bet is to complete her growth by becoming a mother, too. To be a "mother" becomes the premise of her positive identity. Furthermore, it is an identity over which no one else has control.

The meaning of the baby, therefore, may have as much, if not more, to do with the enhancement of the girl's identity as it does with the creation of a new human being. In view of the significance of the baby as the glue and prospective salvation of the mother-daughter dyad, it is clear that the baby is unlikely to be adequately nurtured. Thus, the baby's birth completes one cycle and sets the stage for a repetition of the cycle of poverty.

WHERE TO BEGIN?

Given the enormity of the problem and the economic and human costs involved, "where to begin?" is not a question to be taken lightly. Our answer: begin by thinking structurally. Family therapists must address themselves to those codes and operations that govern human behavior in systems and result in repetitive patterns.

The cycle of poverty is surely a repetitive pattern, the sources of which are structures in three spheres: institutional, root, and seed. Institutional structures originate outside the family per se, but affect it significantly, both directly and indirectly. Racism and other forms of prejudice that systematically deny economic opportunity to certain groups are the most obvious examples of disabling institutional structures. There are myriad others, however, such as unsafe environments, poor schools, and entangled rules and regulations for gaining access to resources. Institutional structures are repaired through changes in social policies and attitudes, as well as by the introduction of new laws such as those that mandate equal opportunity in minority employment and guaranteed minimum income in public assistance programs.

For the most part, family therapists are notoriously apolitical. They believe that they can independently repair family structures, even though the outcome of therapy with families experiencing the cycle of poverty is greatly influenced by institutional structures. The poor, who have no choice of resources, are never free of the influence of politically formed institutions. Furthermore, political impacts on the cycle of poverty are reciprocal. Lobbyists for the poor have been disillusioned when far-reaching political changes have not interrupted the cycle. Not only must therapists, as agents of change, recognize and embrace the political portion of their activities, but also lawmakers must be aware of the need to address internal family structures. After all, redundancies, dysfunctional repetitive patterns, exist in institutional structures as well. The cycle of poverty itself is a prime example of such a redundancy. That it occurs over a 15-year time span, rather than a 15-second, or 15-minute, or 15-hour time span does not disqualify it.

Root structures originate inside the family and involve most basic family operations. In any living organism or system, roots are the fundamental structures of living growth process, and development is retarded or impaired when the roots are injured or weakened. Because families that perpetuate the cycle of poverty from one generation to the next tend to suffer from impaired root structures, they can be called developmentally skewed families.

Not a great deal is known about the root structures of disadvantaged poor families—what they are, how they originate, and how, in some families, they are thoroughly impaired. In their classic study of low socioeconomic families, Minuchin and Montalvo gave family therapists a basis for further study (1966). These researchers discovered that "families of the slums" share "a style of thinking, coping, communicating, and behaving, aspects of which can be directly traced to the structure and processes of the family systems to which they are, or were, a part" (p. 193). Their assertion is that certain families as a group suffer actual and distinctive limitations in the way affect is experienced. As the parents have difficulty distinguishing what they feel themselves, they are unable to help their children communicate and attain what they need. In these observations, Minuchin and his colleagues alluded to root structures.

Skewed root structures produce what Kantor called "negative identity claims" (1980). Unlike "positive identity claims" that are incompletely realized, these negative constructions saturate the outlook of individuals and families and contain within them little possibility for change by current treatment methods. Damage to root structures pervades all levels of functioning. A pattern of affect hunger, for example, is an injured root structure that can result in many dysfunctional sequences. A mother, unsure of her ability to "hold on" to a man, allows him to abuse her child sexually; the child, unsure of and hungry for her mother's love, accepts the abuse. All three in this too familiar scenario are looking for the same thing, and all three are lacking a code of behavior that enables them to obtain what they need.

As Minuchin (1967) implied, another commonly impaired root structure in these families is the ability to differentiate affect. When feelings of desire and aggression are fused, the resulting structures perpetuate cycles of dependence and abuse.

Certain family processes and patterns are more immediately responsible than others for the reproduction and propagation of the basic, even sociogenetic, code of the family system. These are referred to as seeding structures. The phenomenon in which men come and go in a disadvantaged poor family is part of a seeding structure. Because of the mother's low expectation of her ability to secure a man and be satisfied, the man is seen as insignificant. The dynamics of the family system then conspire to block him from forming important relationships with the children, and they learn to expect nothing; the cycle continues.

Seeding structures have become familiar to family therapists because they are associated with the problems and symptoms that require treatment. Alcoholism itself is not a seeding structure; what is, is a pattern that seems to develop in some families where alcoholism is present, where the mother covertly supports (or openly joins) the father in his alcoholism and forces a child (most often a girl) into a parental role. Such children learn to maintain disablement in their families of origin and, by marrying alcoholics, they regenerate the seeding structure in their own families.

Much of what is considered successful in family therapy gains such credit because the treatment changes some undesirable behavior, even in family patterns and often in a relatively short course of therapy. Such changes are not significant, however, unless a seeding structure has been altered. A therapy that achieves symptom relief by removing a grandmother from her too powerful position in relation to her daughter and problem grandson cannot be considered significant in these terms until the seeding structure in which the boy is triangulated into the unresolved issues of his parents is addressed.

When the family's resources are reasonably adequate, that is, when root structures are relatively unimpaired and when the family has access to resources outside its boundaries, family therapists enjoy the luxury of a wide margin of error. With families that have access to good schools, stimulating jobs, and personally enhancing aesthetic experiences, therapy becomes significant because institutional and root structures act as compensatory backup for completion of the process. When resources are scarce, both inside and outside the family, the story is very different indeed. Impaired root and institutional structures undermine therapists' best efforts with this population, trivialize their mediocre efforts, and ridicule their worst and least informed efforts. There is little choice but to direct therapeutic efforts toward diagnosing and treating the seeding structures that are the major sources of maladaptive evolutionary process in these families.

THERAPY AT THE FAMILY CENTER

Typical of the families we see at The Family Center are the Devoes. When we treated them, Marianne was 13 years old. Her mother, Mary, was 30 but looked 40. At home were three younger siblings: John, 8; Patrick, 7; and Denise, 3. Marianne's 15-year-old brother, Rick, was in foster care because his behavior was uncontrollable at home and at school; he had committed minor law violations that eventuated in car theft. Two, or perhaps three, fathers were responsible for the five children, but none was presently living in the apartment. Rick's father, however, lived only two units away in the same housing project, with a 20-year-old woman and her two children. Gino, Mary's current boyfriend, came and went. When he was there, Mary and Gino drank steadily; when he was gone, she was a "wreck." Marianne had not attended school for 2 years. Coolly, stubbornly, she refused to go. She smiled in defiance of the threatening judge and remained steadfastly school-resistant.

The Devoes were brought to the attention of The Family Center by a nurse in the health center that serves the project neighborhood. Mary, in one of her "down" periods, was being treated for physical complaints. A member of The Family Center's outreach team saw the family initially at the health clinic, with the nurse who arranged the informal referral. The mother had also been observed by another member of our staff through her participation in the privately funded Women's Writing Project, a community venture representative of those we support as vehicles for political and structural change.

We chose to use a strategic team with the Devoes and to focus on the structure of Marianne's school resistance. Because mother and daughter seemed to be the important dyad in this structure, we concentrated our efforts on that subsystem after an initial whole family session. Mary and Marianne had fully cooperated in all treatment programs to which they had been exposed in the past, and they cooperated in this one also.

Using techniques representative of brief strategic therapy, and some unconventional ones, the team approached its goal by the 7th session of an 8-session contract. In this session, Marianne and Mary were told not to rush things too much. Marianne was told to hold out even longer than she felt was necessary for the one day a week that she was remaining at home; Mary, who twice that week had been out with girlfriends, was cautioned about enjoying herself too much. As the team congratulated itself, mother and daughter announced a "minor crisis." Mary reported that, while she had been out with her girlfriends, Marianne had gotten drunk with the boys and was "screwing around." As their fight escalated, the team behind the one-way mirror became divided.

Some viewed the flare-up in Marianne's behavior as a distraction and wanted to continue working to consolidate Marianne's return to school.

One member of the team felt strongly that the girl was giving a clear warning of an imminent pregnancy and that the team was treating the right dyad, but the wrong structure to interrupt the cyclical patterns of poverty. In these terms, the success of Marianne's return to school was seen as insignificant.

The team decided to turn its attention to the overreactive relationship between mother and daughter. Insufficient, suffused with anger and longing, it seemed about to redeem itself in the way of generations of disadvantaged poor. We have on videotape a 10-minute segment of Mary and Marianne alone in the therapy room. They approach each other and veer away. Marianne calls her mother's attention to her developing body ("This skirt is too tight!"), and her mother criticizes the way her hair is combed. They sit together briefly on the same couch; Mary comments on Marianne in a way that could almost be considered tender, but within 1 minute their escalating battle propels Marianne from the room.

The decision to treat this seed structure opened a Pandora's box. Behind the collaboration to produce a child lay badly damaged root structures of communication and nurturance, as well as severely deficient institutional structures. No fatherly instructor engaged Marianne at school to take pride in her identity as "student" in a way that could compete with her perception of her identity as "mother." Mary had no other model to offer her daughter and little incentive anywhere else in her environment to look for more from life than the serial satisfaction of need within chronic deprivation.

This case raises the question that is central to the program at The Family Center: Do we focus on symptom relief, or is our greatest commitment to alter the cycle of poverty? In the case of the Devoes, for example, we might opt to treat a seeding structure that would overlook Marianne's immediate needs in favor of starting a healthier cycle for her younger siblings. A process to interrupt the cycle of poverty must address many structures that impinge upon the family, and therapists must change their notions of their power to effect change by brief treatment methods. Technology can be used, however, to make efficient interventions. The Family Center has developed some principles of treatment that are designed to alter the structures that perpetuate the problem economically.

Lend Support to Local Programs; Do Not Start New Ones

Very often, we collaborate with community projects that are quietly engaged in programs to deal with the very structures we want to treat.

Because they approach people's lives realistically and are often task-oriented, they add supports and opportunities for growth that family therapists alone cannot provide. On the other hand, without the responsiveness therapists offer toward family forces that insidiously undermine their best efforts, these programs often fail to maintain their initial gains.

In the housing project where the Devoes live, volunteers staff an after-school tutoring program called The Children's Writing Center. There, with individual attention, John Devoe learns, writes, and creates. The project seems to succeed where the school fails. A staff person from The Family Center is able to appraise the children's center staff of John's family situation, which threatens to undo his gains. John's energies are caught up by his mother's changing moods as Gino comes and goes, and she feels more or less successful as a woman. Aware of John's burdensome responsibility to be attentive to his mother, the tutor can help him to mobilize the scarce resources he has left for ordinary 8-year-old learning.

Make Seeding Structures, Not Symptoms and Crises, the Focus of Treatment

Frequently, a family undergoes multiple crises. Some therapists are tempted to help the family solve each crisis as it comes; ironically, however, it may appear that crises proliferate to meet the willingness of helpers to resolve them. Crises exist as a matter of course in the disadvantaged poor population. The therapist who hopes to solve them is only invited to share the exhausting experience the family knows so well.

Therapists should not, of course, ignore symptoms and crises, but they should realize that treating them may be insignificant in terms of structural change. When a mother brings in a 5-year-old child who shows signs of sexual molestation and blames her absent lover, the child's safety must be ensured. The seeding structure that must be addressed to save the next generation of girl children is the low expectation the mother has about men.

Do Not Try to Become the Missing Link in the Damaged Structure

Some therapists may want to become the stable nurturer or parent in treating the families. When family root structures are intact, it is sometimes possible to provide a "corrective experience" that can further whatever healthy development has been temporarily derailed. Such a family may learn new possibilities by risking affective and communicational leaps that otherwise would be unsafe. In a family with impaired root structures, however, the therapist's "corrective presence" finds no resonance to generate new structures. The therapist becomes, in effect, a transient gratification. The dysfunctional structure remains untouched, while the therapist is consumed.

Do Not Forget that Giving is a Complicated Structural Business

One of the pitfalls of the housing project as an institution is that it must cast a lifeline to the poor. A structure is created whereby the giving inadvertently reinforces the dependency that is common to the culture of poverty. The giving may be essential (e.g., money, food, services), but it is neither nurturing nor rewarding—thus, it does not address the basic needs of affect or competency (power). The recipient is chosen in an undifferentiated way, reminiscent of the undifferentiated responses commonly seen among clients as they relate to their children or friends. Dependency and helplessness are exacerbated by the ephemeral nature of the giving; it does not depend on a particular attribute or action of the recipient. It is also out of the recipient's control, unless manipulative measures are developed to gain some measure of control. Therefore, the therapist who enters the family in a naive giving mode may be reinforcing an unproductive institutional structure. Interventions should alter the notion of giving from a one-way give-and-take situation to an interactive sharing and exchange that initiates a new seeding structure. In its programs at the housing projects, The Family Center staff involve parents as helpers and colleagues in the operations of children's groups. As the program develops, mothers will be engaged as experts on aspects of their children's behavior and will be invited, even expected, to participate in the ongoing development of projects. As parents perform these tasks, they will be rewarded according to their achievement and success.

Be Aware of the Politics of Interventions

When a 13-year-old boy assumes the prerogatives of a parent over his younger siblings in a female-headed poor household, the situation may be labeled an upset hierarchy or, to the contrary, an adaptive reconstruction. A therapist who intervenes to right the hierarchy would have totally misunderstood the vitality and fittingness of the boy's role, given the Gestalt of all the structures that make up his experience.

For as long as Marianne remained disabled and refused to go to school, her mother received a special allotment from welfare. As the therapy approached its goal, Mary informed the therapist that her funds would be terminated unless she attended a job training program. Mary, who had never worked and was terrified of the prospect, appealed to the therapist to intervene. In the case of the 13-year-old parental child, the politics of intervention are subtle. In the dilemma that Mary Devoe imposed on her therapist, they are not.

Create a Self-Sustaining Network to Develop Structural Change

Families that are making significant changes in their habitual patterns as a result of therapy may find themselves isolated and ostracized from the community. Whatever its shortcomings, the culture of poverty provides membership in a group. When families free themselves from these blinding structures, they also relinquish group membership. If they feel they have nowhere to go, changes, however significant and gratifying, are likely to be whittled away by pressures from the existing culture. There is no solution but to find new structures or to create a new institutional framework to serve at least as an interim alternative to that which has been relinquished so that gains made within the family can be sustained and supported.

There are certainly efforts being made to provide these interim structures in the housing projects. The Family Center is developing or collaborating with others to develop a children's group and a mothers' group. The children's group is a place where children can get reinforcement for adhering to the boundaries and to the consistent rules that are replacing random direction at home as the family evolves new structures. It is a place where successes are possible and rewarded. Competency is developed as expectations become clear. Nurturing from leaders (who are sometimes mothers) and from each other replaces noise and struggle for attention. The children's group is an ''interim'' program devised not to provide what is missing in the family, but to provide an external supportive structure for what is developing at home.

The mothers' group is based on the same principle. It provides a network to support new identities as they emerge. It is a place where mothers can deal with deficits in affect, competency, and communication. Because the structures involved are deep and significant, intervention requires a great deal of time. The group has the potential of longevity, mutual growth, and support with the rewarding of success and the ability to accept new therapists to help them complete the intervention process.

CONCLUSION

All the activities described are focused on what is sometimes perceived as an impossible task—bringing a halt to the cycle of poverty. In our efforts to repair dysfunctional structures, we try to identify those phenomena that are most likely to be passed to the next generation. We design interventions and work within other programs to create healthier models. There are few shortcuts. Sometimes we need, as much for our own morale as for program gain, to devise remedies that seem to have immediate results. Families also need to see something happen. We cannot say we have succeeded, however, until we have broken the cycle that passes from generation to generation.

REFERENCES

Kantor, D. Critical identity image: A concept linking individual, couple and family development. In J.K. Pearce & L.J. Friedman (Eds.), *Family therapy: Combining psychodynamic and family systems approaches*. New York: Grune & Stratton, 1980.

Minuchin, S., & Montalvo, B. An approach for diagnosis of the low socioeconomic family. *Psychiatric Research Report 20, American Psychiatric Association*, February 1966.

Minuchin, S., et al. *Families of the slums*. New York: Basic Books, 1967.

Minuchin, S., & Montalvo, B. Techniques for working with disorganized low socioeconomic families. In J. Haley (Ed.), *Changing families*. New York: Grune & Stratton, 1971.

Peacock, C.A. *Hand-me-down dreams*. New York: Schochen Books, 1981.

6. Working with Latin American Families

Ena Vazquez-Nuttall, EdD
Associate Professor
University of Massachusetts
Amherst, Massachusetts

Zoila Avila-Vivas, MA, CAGS
Doctoral Candidate
University of Massachusetts
Amherst, Massachusetts

Gisela Morales-Barreto, MA
Doctoral Candidate
University of Massachusetts
Amherst, Massachusetts

THE CHALLENGE

MORE AND MORE OFTEN, MENTAL HEALTH PRACTITIONERS ARE FACING the challenge of working with children and families of different cultures (Falicov, 1982; Garcia-Preto, 1982). Official 1976 counts of the National Center for Education Statistics and the Bureau of the Census (Bell, 1982) revealed that an estimated 28 million people in the United States had backgrounds in languages other than English. Of these, approximately 5.8 million were school-aged children, 4 to 18. The largest language minority group was and is the Spanish-speaking group, and this population is expected to increase in the future at a more rapid rate than the population of language majority children. Since Latin American children are referred for psychological services more frequently than are majority children (Canino, Earley, & Rogler, 1980), family therapists must be prepared to treat them.

Latin American families present a challenge to the family therapist, not only because they are linguistically and culturally different, but also because they share the multiple problems associated with poverty. The majority of Latin American families are undereducated, unemployed or poorly paid, poorly housed, and poorly served by the health care system (Padilla, 1981). The case of Mrs. Rodriguez illustrates some of the multiple problems typically faced by Latin American families living in the United States.

Mrs. Rodriguez is a Puerto Rican single parent trying to bring up a family of 11 children. Because she has only a third-grade education and speaks very little English, she frequently depends on her children to serve as interpreters, even though their English is poor. The family is on welfare. While several of the older children are married and live away from home, six are still at home and attend school. At one time or another, most of the children have experienced difficulties in school. Luis, one of the oldest boys, quit school last year and is presently unemployed. Pablo, a high-school junior, was suspended from school because of excessive tardiness, absenteeism, and drug use in the classroom. Mario, who attends junior high school, was taken to court because he was found sexually abusing a classmate in one of the school bathrooms. Maria, the youngest child, is several years behind in reading. Mrs. Rodriguez is presently seriously depressed, uncertain whether to continue her struggle or return to Puerto Rico. Although cooperative and progressive, the school system does not provide a bilingual education program. The community does not have any social agencies with family therapists who can speak Spanish. The school is becoming concerned about the large amount of resources being dedicated to this one family's problems.

Unfortunately, too many school systems lack appropriate bilingual staff, which exacerbates the problems of language minority children and makes it difficult to offer meaningful help. Latin American parents who try to establish contact with these schools experience frustration. Not only are written and oral communications often in a language parents cannot understand (Montalvo, 1974), but there is little, if any, effort to orient these parents to the American school system, behaviors expected of children and parents, and services available. This gap in understanding contributes to the children's high dropout rates, low academic achievement, and low career and college aspirations. These children also suffer from a higher than average frequency of sleep and articulation problems, physical problems, inadequate intellectual development, anxiety and fear, anger and belligerence, agitation and hyperactivity, and antisocial attitudes (Canino et al., 1980).

In spite of the highly stressful situations in which they find themselves, Latin Americans in the United States are less likely than is the general population to seek psychotherapy or counseling services (Abad, Ramos, & Boyce, 1974; Badillo-Ghali, 1977). In addition to the socioeconomic and language barriers, Latin American families are held back by characteristics of their own unique culture, such as their reliance on the extended family support system rather than on agencies, a religious belief that God will take care of them, a trust in faith healers, and distorted perceptions about mental health and illness (Ruiz & Padilla, 1977). Referrals by the schools to mental health agencies are thus more common than self-referrals. The role of the therapist in many of these cases is to try to connect the family and the school, educating parents about the rules and expectations of the school staff, and educating school staff about the parents' values.

TRADITIONAL CULTURAL VALUES OF THE LATIN AMERICAN FAMILY

The basic cultural values of Latin American families must be understood by any therapist attempting to work with them. While each family, of course, has its own idiosyncrasies and each Latin American country has its own variations on the theme, these traditional values have to some extent been shared by them all.

Familismo

Latin American cultures traditionally place a preeminent value on *familismo*, or family orientation, as the major source of identity, cohesiveness, and support. Family members look first to the family to meet their needs and to facilitate the resolution of conflicts (Avila-Vivas, Morales-Barreto, Russ, & Vazquez-Nuttall, 1983; Christensen, 1977). This family orientation includes not only the nuclear family, but also members of the extended family, close family friends, and *padrinos* (godparents). In fact, the term *familia* (family) implies extended family kin or combinations of individual households. *La casa* (home) refers to the nuclear family.

It is not easy for individuals to detach themselves emotionally and acquire a sense of self-identity in a culture that stresses dependency and overprotection, demands loyalty from its members, and subordinates individual needs to family needs and interests (Falicov, 1982). Using the terminology of structural family therapy, the normal pattern in Latin American families is enmeshment (Canino & Canino, 1980). Therapists should keep in mind the cultural normalcy of this pattern in order to avoid misconceptions and misdiagnosis (Garcia-Preto, 1982). A knowledge of familismo makes it easy for a therapist to understand why a family might bring 12 members to a family therapy session. It also makes a therapist appreciate the following situation:

> A Latin American family was sent to a therapist because the 12-year-old daughter was frequently absent from school and the principal thought the parents were irresponsible. Upon questioning, the therapist determined that the parents kept the child home when the grandmother was ill, when anniversaries and birthdays were celebrated, and when the mother needed help caring for the younger children.

Personalismo

In Latin American families, there is an emphasis on *personalismo*, as opposed to a depersonalized life style (Canino & Canino, 1980). Personalismo also calls for individualized contact and attention in all social, economic, and political relations (Mintz, 1966). For example, in school, Latin American children will expect and appreciate individual attention from the teacher and significant others. They will do better if the teacher asks them personal questions about members of their families and other personal matters. In therapy, families will also do better if there is a warm rapport with the therapist rather than a more distant analytic approach.

Fatalismo

The literature indicates that the Latin American family has a fatalistic view of life and tends to be present-oriented, since it feels powerless to control the future (Garcia-Preto, 1982; Ruiz & Padilla, 1977). The poorer the family, the more likely it is to accept whatever happens as part of its fate (Mintz, 1966). Poor Latin American parents tend to pay little attention to developmental milestones in their children, resigning themselves uncomplainingly to any irregularities or handicaps as the will of God. Anglo-American teachers and therapists should thus not be surprised if a developmental lag has not been recognized by the parents.

Marianismo and Machismo

In the poor Latin American family, women are traditionally idealized as pure and self-sacrificing, like the Virgin Mary. Overprotection of girls to save their virginity is a normal component of the culture (Falicov, 1982). Men, on the other hand, are traditionally supposed to be macho. They are expected to be authoritarian, dominating, and aggressive, constantly seeking sexual satisfaction. The strong macho character brings to the family pride, respect, loyalty, and protection (Garcia-Preto, 1982; Mizio, 1974).

Traditionally, women are expected to remain under the authority and control of men. The need for women to enter the labor force because of financial conditions has produced a change in the low socioeconomic Latin American family, however, and a more egalitarian structure has emerged in the marital subsystem (Canino & Canino, 1980).

Respeto and Dignidad

Latin American family members are expected to have respect for authority, the family, and tradition (Christensen, 1977). Dignity is a source of pride and self-worth.

Respect is reinforced through traditional hierarchical patterns in the family. Latin American parents tend to set a certain amount of distance between themselves and their children. The patriarchal father, particularly, is likely to be more distant and less communicative, while the matriarchal, care-giving mother tends to be closer and more affectionate with the children

(Canino & Canino, 1980). Respect for parents extends also to other authority figures, such as teachers, older neighbors, and relatives. As a respectful sign, children are taught to look down when being scolded by parents or authority figures. This nonverbal attitude can be misinterpreted as disrespect by a teacher or other authority figure who is not acquainted with the culture.

Espiritismo

Many Latin American families subscribe to *espiritismo*, the belief that there is an invisible universe populated with spirits who can influence the behavior of people in positive and negative ways. These spirits may be people who have died, people who have yet to be born, or beings in a process of reincarnation.

While anyone may be aware of spirits, some people are thought to develop *facultades* (psychic faculties) that enable them to control the visible world by operating through the universe of spirits. These mediums represent a unique mental health resource for Latin American families (Rogler & Hollingshead, 1965). Working either with individuals or with groups as large as 15 to 20 people, a medium interprets symptoms and problems as the work of evil spirits or as *pruebas* (challenges) that the person will have to meet. By postulating external reasons for problems, in terms of curses, spirits, and challenges, the medium obviates guilt or blame in the family.

The belief in espiritismo is found in all classes of Latin American society and is a major source of meaning in life. A therapist aware of the Latin American belief in espiritismo would understand an adolescent girl who listened to the voice of her dead grandmother as a respite from school problems. The therapist would not label her schizophrenic.

THE FAMILY TREATMENT PROCESS

Referrals from the School

Latin American families are often referred to a mental health facility only after several intervention attempts have failed. A teacher who observes a child's behavior problems at school and believes that the child is showing emotional instability or suffering from parental abuse generally tries first to approach the parents directly. This is seldom a successful strategy for a number of reasons, however. Impoverished Latin American parents may feel threatened by school personnel and fear adverse reactions to their poor

English, cultural values, or child-rearing practices. In addition, these parents generally do not recognize the value of home-school interaction, believing instead that school personnel are the educational authorities and know what is best for their children. The school psychologist is also apt to be identified as part of the school system and viewed in the same way. A family therapy approach is most appropriate and should appeal to Latin American families because of their marked investment in family life. As stated by Mizio (1974) and supported by Christensen (1977), "the [Latin American] family must be helped to utilize its own strengths, to draw upon its humanitarian values and to support its kin" (p. 83).

Assignment of the Case to an Appropriate Therapist

The therapist appropriate for Latin American families has an understanding of Latin American culture, a sensitivity to the needs of these families, and an ability to communicate in the families' preferred language. While some families may prefer an Anglo therapist who can introduce them to the majority culture, other families can communicate only in Spanish. The therapist who resorts to using an interpreter must be aware of limitations. For one, it is a rare interpreter who can adequately convey an interaction to all parties. Translations generally misrepresent the true meaning and cultural significance of family expressions and fail to consider nonverbal behaviors. The greatest difficulty occurs when children must interpret for their parents. In the Latin American family, which places a premium on respect for parental authority, the child-interpreter might be seen as insubordinately intruding on adult issues (Canino & Canino, 1980). Possible solutions to the language problem are to work with a cotherapist who speaks Spanish or to train Spanish-speaking members of the community to be paraprofessional assistants.

Initial Contact with the Mental Health Agency

To make Latin American families feel comfortable and welcome, agencies are well advised to have objects and symbols of Latin American culture in the waiting rooms and offices (Bernal & Flores-Ortiz, 1982). Pamphlets and other educational information should be available in Spanish. If possible, the agency's clerical personnel should greet family members in their own language, offering clear directions and answering questions (Abad et al., 1974). Convenient locations, time schedules, transportation, and child care are also priorities for agencies that provide services to this population.

Joining Phase

The therapist's effort to make the family feel comfortable and to explain the process of therapy is particularly important with Latin American families, who are known to drop therapy if their first impressions of the therapeutic relationship are not positive. As Minuchin (1974) noted, the therapist should provide support to the family without seeking to change it and should accommodate to the family's style and affective range during the joining phase.

A familiarity with Latin American social customs is important. For instance, Latin Americans all stand up for greetings; men or younger persons extend their hands first. Latin Americans generally use two last names—their father's as well as their mother's—and neither should be omitted (as in the name Juan *Perez Martinez*). In addition, Latin Americans maintain less space between parties in social interactions and are more expressive about emotions than Anglo-Americans. Conversation is accompanied by abundant body language and facial expressions.

A friendly and social atmosphere at the beginning of each therapy session is helpful in establishing a relationship of confidence and rapport (Bernal & Flores-Ortiz, 1982; Mizio, 1974). Some authors recommend the use of humor, proverbs, and metaphors in engaging the family, but warn that the therapist must also appear competent, firm, and respectful (Bluestone & Vela, 1982). The therapist should expect Latin Americans to ask personal questions and should be prepared to respond briefly without inquiring about the motivation behind the question (Mizio, 1974).

It is particularly important to respect customs based on family hierarchical patterns in order to "convey to the family that their culturally prescribed roles and rules are not being challenged at the outset of therapy" (Bernal & Flores-Ortiz, 1982, p. 358). For example, the family therapist should not speak first to a child. The father, if present, should be addressed initially, since he has the major authority in the family. If the father is reluctant to participate in discussions, the therapist can sometimes reduce his anxiety by commenting that his presence at the session shows he cares very much for his family. The therapist can then make a direct request for his invaluable help.

Early in therapy, it is important to determine the family members' expectations of the therapeutic process and their understanding of mental health. The low-income Latin American family often comes to therapy with a set of expectations based on previous experiences with other health or social agencies, or with spiritualists. Some might therefore expect similar treatment interventions (e.g., physical examinations, drug prescriptions, direct advice, contact with spirits) for the present difficulties (Abad et al., 1974; Bluestone & Vela, 1982). Throughout therapy, it may be necessary for the therapist to assume the role of an educator, instructing the family in the nature of emotional discomfort and the ways in which therapy differs from other interventions (Bluestone & Vela, 1982; Mizio, 1974). At the same time, the therapist should be learning about the family's cultural uniqueness and difficulties in adapting to the majority culture. Families are usually eager to discuss this subject, and the topic can help to shift the focus away from the identified patient into the family context, thus facilitating family change.

The more therapists know about the family and its culture, the less likely they are to perceive general cultural traits as idiosyncrasies of the particular family.

Assessment of the Family

As the therapist begins to assess a Latin American family system, it is important to recognize the conflict between traditional Latin American family values and the new culture in which the family is trying to function, often at the lowest socioeconomic level.

Typical Acculturation Conflicts

Some family conflicts clearly can be traced to the impact of acculturation (Mizio, 1974). For instance, the Latin American male in the United States does not get *respeto* and *dignidad*. Traditional *machismo* and *marianismo* roles are not valued (Badillo-Ghali, 1977). The mother who places great importance on her daughter's virginity is likely to be labeled old-fashioned and overprotective. Latin American socialized behavior of submissiveness and deference to others may be misinterpreted in a society that is accustomed to aggressive behavior. Intergenerational conflicts arise in a social context that emphasizes independence instead of *familismo*, and children's negative reactions to their parents' values and to school might be an expression of their resentment for being looked down upon by their peer group.

Family from a Developmental Perspective

Characteristic issues that are associated with the different life stages of low-income Latin American families in the United States have a strong impact on a child's school behavior and achievement. It is thus important to identify the family's life stage and to assess the sources of support the family has as it encounters stresses and crises (Colon, 1980; Minuchin, 1974). Colon (1980) postulated three distinctive life stages of the low-income multiproblem Latin American family. In the first stage, adolescents are either pushed out of the home to learn to survive by themselves or initially retained by the family as a potential source of income. In either case, many young men soon leave the family and attach themselves to a peer group that consists of high-school dropouts who believe that illegal activity is the remedy for their poverty. Those adolescents who are able to take advantage of education and job opportunities usually find that their success leads to feelings of guilt for leaving their families and peers behind (Colon, 1980). The girls' only option may seem to be to attach themselves to a male figure and achieve their identity through motherhood.

In the second stage, the young couple enters into a relationship (married or unmarried) that is inherently unstable (Colon, 1980). With the advent of children, the mother usually becomes the central figure in the home, financially aided by welfare, and the father becomes peripheral. The mother becomes overburdened by the children and suffers from tension and anxiety (Vazquez-Nuttall & Nuttall, 1979). In an attempt to help the mother, one of the children, usually the oldest, takes the role of the parental child. This child either becomes the object of sibling rage because the child has inadequate parenting skills and power (Colon, 1980; Minuchin, 1974) or becomes the idealized sibling because the child shows unlimited care and support throughout the life cycle. This parental child may become enraged at the mother for failing to be an adequate parent, however (Minuchin, 1974). When the father stays at home with the children while the mother works, he is likely to feel inadequate because his male authority is reduced (Mizio, 1974). In some cases, the parents remain juveniles and avoid responsibilities; then their children, especially their sons, grow up without adequate parental role models and are unable to visualize their future family roles (Colon, 1980).

During the third stage ("later life"), a grandmother sometimes makes a grandchild another one of her own children; the mother thus remains a daughter and the new child considers her an older sister instead of a mother.

In the midst of these highly dysfunctional family patterns, children are likely to present school-related problems. Instead of supporting their children's school activities, these parents are more apt to add to their children's burden with unrealistic demands or neglect. Many parents also fail to set limits that enable their children to behave in a socialized way in the structured environment of the school.

Family's Degree of Connectedness with Latin American Culture

In identifying the family's problems and planning a course of treatment, the therapist should determine the degree to which the family is connected to the Latin American culture and the degree to which family members are interested in assimilating to the Anglo-American culture (Bernal & Flores-Ortiz, 1982; Padilla, 1981). Helpful areas to explore are

- the importance of ethnic values and traditions to the family
- the existence of intergenerational cultural strains
- the importance of celebrating holidays and religious feasts
- the extent to which the family relies on institutions in the neighborhood
- the family's perception of the role that schools play in a child's acculturation

This evaluation intervention is also very helpful in identifying the cultural and relational resources available to the family in the community.

Boundaries of the Family System

During the joining stage, the therapist should regard the child who has been identified as the patient by the school as the one "who is expressing in the most visible way, a problem affecting the entire system" (Minuchin, 1974, p. 129). To determine the boundaries of the system, it is helpful to give the family the opportunity to decide who is part of the family system and who is to be included in the family session. Family maps are useful resources in this regard (Minuchin, 1974).

When a child has school-related problems, it might be useful to include the teacher in some sessions. The therapist could suggest this idea to the family as a positive strategy that would help the teacher to become more sensitive to the family's culture and the child's difficulties. This approach would lay the groundwork for closer relationships between the family and the school in the future.

The Therapeutic Contract

The therapist must listen to what the family identifies as problems and must not assume that certain issues are sources of conflict or stress because of the family's acculturation process or value system (Christensen, 1977). In explaining the treatment process to the family, the therapist should be specific about the logistics of treatment, including the location (e.g., office, home, school) and schedule. Latin Americans tend not to value promptness, and there might be some problems in keeping appointment times. Also, because they often view mental health care as crisis-oriented, attendance might deteriorate as the situation improves. These factors need to be closely monitored (Bluestone & Vela, 1982).

The treatment plan should be coordinated with other services the family is receiving in order to avoid a fragmentation of services that could exacerbate the family's disorganization. The school and the welfare department should be consulted on a regular basis (Hardy-Fanta & MacMahon-Herrera, 1981). Regular use of the school setting as a context for therapy helps the family learn about the school system and feel more comfortable in establishing a relationship with school personnel.

At the end of the preliminary phase of treatment, the therapist should give the family members some feedback about their dynamics and difficulties. Their efforts in attempting to resolve difficulties in spite of their overwhelming life circumstances should be acknowledged with praise and understanding.

An Ecostructural Approach to Treatment

The ecostructural approach has been developed as a culturally sensitive model of treatment for poor Latin American families (Scopetta & King, 1976; Vazquez-Nuttall & Nuttall, 1979). On the one hand, it is based on ecological theory in which the family is viewed as a system in continuous interaction with other systems within the larger realm of society. On the other hand, it draws upon Minuchin's structural theory in which the family is studied in terms of its own system, subsystems, hierarchy, and generational boundaries (Minuchin, 1974). Using the ecostructural approach, "the locus of [a] conflict can be found in the dysfunctional transactions of the family with other societal systems, and/or in the transactions within the family" (Scopetta & King, 1976, p. 5). The therapist is active and directive, operating at the interface between the family and other systems.

Latin American families seem to respond well to therapy models such as the ecostructural model; not only are they active, short-term, and oriented to the present and to problem resolution, but also they allow for the flexibility of crisis intervention and drop-in visits (Abad et al., 1974).

As therapists begin to intervene in the family system, they may suggest alternative ways for family members to interact and resolve conflicts. The goal should be to create a flexible balance between autonomy and interdependency (Minuchin, 1974; Scopetta & King, 1976). The spouse subsystem should be clearly defined and protected from outside intrusion. The parental subsystem should be helped to perform its executive functions, such as setting limits for the children, without relying on an extended family member or child. The children subsystem should be differentiated with appropriate rights, privileges, and obligations for different ages. The sibling subsystem should have the opportunity to learn cooperation, competition, and other skills necessary for living with peers in society (Hardy-Fanta & MacMahon-Herrera, 1981).

As changes are introduced, conflicts of loyalty can develop among family members who have a strong commitment to closeness, even if separated by geographical distances. It is crucial for the therapist to help family members accommodate to their new relationships. It is also important to ensure that the family maintains contact with members of the extended family and friends, particularly during periods of loneliness and rootlessness.

During intervention, therapists must be careful not to undermine parental authority by establishing coalitions with the children against the parents. This would alienate the therapist from the parents and destroy all possibility of further positive family intervention (Mizio, 1974).

Therapists should also be attuned to the varying degrees of acculturation among the different members of the family and be prepared to ease the intergenerational conflicts that often ensue. Parents who fear that they will become alienated from their more rapidly acculturated children, for example, sometimes accelerate their own acculturation dysfunctionally or try to suppress the process in their children.

While a major objective of the ecostructural model is to bring structural order into the family system, it is also intended to have an impact in the community context. Since Latin American families tend to feel somewhat powerless in dealing with external social forces, they need to be taught how to perform these extrafamilial roles (Padilla, 1981) and how to deal effectively with their anger toward social institutions (Canino & Canino, 1980).

Because of the complexity of working with the multiproblem low-income Latin American family, Garcia-Preto (1982) and others have suggested a team approach. This approach allows a variety of clinical interventions and concrete services to be coordinated. Moreover, the team approach resembles and reinforces the Latin American's extended support system.

The case of the Gonzales family illustrates the use of the ecostructural approach with a multiproblem Latin American family.

The Gonzales family was referred for therapy by their daughter Maria's teacher, who was concerned about the 11-year-old child's behavior and suspected some form of neglect by her parents. The therapist was told that the Gonzales family had emigrated from Puerto Rico with the hope of finding better medical and educational opportunities for their handicapped children. Pedrito, 9, has Down's syndrome, and Luis, 6, suffers from epileptic seizures, enuresis, and several other physical problems.

At the time of the referral, Mrs. Gonzales, 29, was a housewife, and her husband, 34, was unemployed. The family was receiving welfare, and their social worker had recently referred the family to another agency for the father's alcohol abuse problems.

Only the mother and children came in for the initial therapy interview. The mother reported that the father had refused to attend the session, saying that any problems were caused by the mother's failure to be assertive enough with their daughter. She reported the father had also expressed his anger about driving his family to care facilities where they did not get any help and where he could not deal with English-speaking providers.

During the assessment phase, the mother told the therapist how depressed and frustrated she was with so much work and so little cooperation from her husband.

It appeared to the therapist during the initial sessions that the daughter, Maria, was taking the role of the parental child in order to help when the mother was depressed. Maria related that she often wanted to play with her friends, but was told to help her mother instead. The mother responded that, as a child, she had been required to do the same things her daughter was doing. She also made it clear that the school's request to meet with her about Maria's problem was only adding to her already very stressed life.

As the therapist evaluated this case, an ecostructural approach appeared to be the appropriate treatment modality. Intervention needed to focus on both the family system and the external environment. The family system needed restructuring by redefining the weakened parental subsystem, by strengthening the spouse subsystem, and by restoring the daughter to the sibling subsystem where she could enjoy activities appropriate to her age, while still helping her parents.

The family also needed immediate assistance in dealing with external systems. Medical and psychological care for the family was centered on one agency. The father, after being convinced by the therapist that his presence was invaluable in helping the family, joined an alcoholism rehabilitation program. The mentally retarded child, who had previously not received any special assistance, was placed in a program for children with special needs. Further planned interventions were summer camp for Maria and a women's self-help group for the mother. The therapist also took an active role in serving as a connection between the family and social service agencies.

Termination of the Therapeutic Relationship

When approaching closure in treatment, the therapist should be sensitive to the difficulty the family may have in severing a relationship with someone who may now be perceived as a member of the extended family. The family should be given the options of remaining in contact with the therapist and consulting in times of crisis or need. If possible, the therapist should implement a follow-up process to inquire about the family's progress periodically and should keep in touch with the school and other external agencies with which the family might be involved.

The follow-up process should have a preventive aspect. Supplemental programs, such as remedial education, vocational guidance, drug abuse and crime prevention programs, nutrition and health programs, home management programs, and social management programs (e.g., on welfare and taxes), should be provided by the community agency (Padilla, 1981) to promote health in the family rather than dwelling exclusively on a treatment orientation. In addition, cultural programs, such as art exhibits, films, and concerts, help to strengthen the community and establish the agency as a trusted source of continuing support (Ruiz & Padilla, 1977).

Ideally, as the family leaves treatment, it should be able to function effectively as an open and flexible system (Scopetta & King, 1976) with the capacity for development and growth of its members and the ability to maintain satisfying bonds within the social system.

INFERENCES FOR OTHER LANGUAGE MINORITY GROUPS

It is always important for a therapist to understand a family's language, culture, and values. While Latin American families value family cohesiveness and face-to-face contact, families from other cultures may value self-restraint, individualism, nature, or academic achievement. These values must be respected, not diagnosed as pathological because they may differ from those of the majority culture. The therapist should also seek to understand the acculturation conflicts the family experiences as it tries to adapt to the majority culture and should make an effort to help ease the transition.

The treatment modality that is chosen should complement not only the family's cultural values, but also their socioeconomic problems. The eco-structural approach has been recommended for dealing with low-income families that encounter continuing problems with schools, housing, and employment. The challenge of dealing with language minority families can be met if the therapist acquires the needed cultural and linguistic knowledge and maintains a sensitive respect for other cultures.

REFERENCES

Abad, V., Ramos, J., & Boyce, E. A model for delivery of mental health services to Spanish-speaking minorities. *American Journal of Orthopsychiatry*, 1974, *44*(4), 584–595.

Avila-Vivas, Z., Morales-Barreto, G., Russ, S., & Vazquez-Nuttall, E. *Training counselors to work with minorities: Myths and realities*. Paper presented at the American Personnel and Guidance Association, Washington, DC, March 1983.

Badillo-Ghali, S. Cultural sensitivity and the Puerto Rican client. *Social Casework*, 1977 *58*(8), 459–468.

Bell, T.H. *The condition of bilingual education in the nation, 1982*. Rosslyn, VA: National Clearinghouse for Bilingual Education, 1982.

Bernal, G., & Flores-Ortiz, Y. Latino families in therapy: Engagement and evaluation. *Journal of Marital and Family Therapy*, 1982, *8*, 357–365.

Bluestone, H., & Vela, R.M. Transcultural aspects in the psychotherapy of the Puerto Rican poor in New York City. *Journal of the American Academy of Psychoanalysis*, 1982, *10*(2), 269–283.

Canino, I., & Canino, G. Impact of stress on the Puerto Rican family: Treatment considerations. *American Journal of Orthopsychiatry*, 1980, *50*(3), 535–541.

Canino, I., Earley, B., & Rogler, L. *The Puerto Rican child in New York City: Stress and mental health*. New York: Hispanic Research Center, Fordham University, 1980.

Christensen, E.W. When counseling Puerto Ricans. *Personnel and Guidance Journal*, 1977, *55*, 412–415.

Colon, F. The family life cycle of the multiproblem poor family. In E. Carter & M. McGoldrick (Eds.), *The family life cycle: A framework for family therapy*. New York: Gardner Press, 1980.

Falicov, C. Mexican families. In M. McGoldrick, J. Pearce, & J. Giordano (Eds.), *Ethnicity and family therapy*. New York: Guilford Press, 1982.

Garcia-Preto, N. Puerto Rican families. In M. McGoldrick, J. Pearce, & J. Giordano (Eds.), *Ethnicity and family therapy*. New York: Guilford Press, 1982.

Hardy-Fanta, C., & MacMahon-Herrera, E. Adapting family therapy to the Hispanic family. *Social Casework*, 1981, *62*, 138–148.

Mintz, S. Puerto Rico: An essay in the definition of a national culture. In *Status of Puerto Rico: Selected background studies*. Paper prepared for the United States-Puerto Rico Commission on the Status of Puerto Rico, 1966.

Minuchin, S. *Families and family therapy*. Cambridge, MA: Harvard University Press, 1974.

Mizio, E. Impact of external systems on the Puerto Rican family. *Social Casework,* 1974, *55,* 76–83.

Montalvo, B. Home-school conflict and the Puerto Rican child. *Social Casework,* 1974, *55,* 100–110.

Padilla, A. Pluralistic counseling and psychotherapy for Hispanic Americans. In A. Marsella, & P. Pedersen (Eds.), *Cross cultural counseling and psychotherapy.* New York: Pergamon Press, 1981.

Rogler, L., & Hollingshead, A. *Trapped: Families and schizophrenia.* New York: John C. Wiley, 1965.

Ruiz, R., & Padilla, A. Counseling Latinos. *Personnel and Guidance Journal,* 1977, *55,* 213–231.

Scopetta, M., & King, O. *An ecostructural family therapy approach to the rehabilitation of the Latino drug abuser: History and development.* Miami, FL: U.S. Department of Health, Education and Welfare, 1976.

Vasquez-Nuttall, E., & Nuttall, R. *Support systems for low income Spanish speaking families.* Paper presented at the American Psychological Association Annual Meeting, New York City, September 1979.

7. Divorced Families and the Schools: An Interface of Systems

Janine M. Bernard, PhD
Purdue University
West Lafayette, Indiana

SCHOOL-RELATED PROBLEMS OF CHILDREN OFTEN EMERGE AS ISSUES during the course of family therapy. Sometimes, the family therapist can initiate solutions within the family system. At other times, it is also necessary for parents to approach and involve the school when problems arise. Although more stressful for the parents, this more inclusive approach benefits the child because it synchronizes home life and school life.

When the parents divorce, this two-pronged approach to treatment is especially important. Both systems (family and school) react to the parental divorce, and the child must cope with these reactions in addition to his or her own reactions. Often, this alone is enough to stimulate a crisis. Even if no problems are apparent, parents should be in contact with the school during divorce to support their child. Family therapists are in an excellent position to recommend such parental involvement.

CHILDREN OF DIVORCE

As central as the topic of divorce has been in child, family, and educational literature, reports are still contradictory and tend to emphasize consequences rather than specific causes within the context of divorce. Recently, Elias (1983) reported a "ground breaking" study conducted at Kent State University of 699 children in 38 states. Preliminary findings showed that

1. Children from divorced families tend to be less popular, have less self-control, and display more fear of failure.
2. They miss more school.
3. Boys consistently fare worse than girls in adjusting to a divorce.
4. These findings hold true regardless of the family's income. (p. 3)

Other studies support these findings. Snyder, Minnick, and Anderson (1980) studied elementary school children (kindergarten through grade 5) and found that girls from divorced families saw the school nurse more often than did other girls. Their complaints were often categorized as psychosomatic or "ill-defined." Boys from divorced families, on the other hand, saw the school nurse less often than did other boys, reinforcing an age-old stereotype about each sex's ability to disclose stress. All children of divorce were involved in significantly more accidents on the playground and elsewhere, however, leading to "trauma" visits to the school nurse.

In a similar study (Brown, 1980), secondary school youngsters from one-parent homes were compared with those from two-parent homes. The adolescents who lived with one parent were disproportionately associated with tardiness, discipline problems, suspensions, changing schools, truancy, Title I participation, dropouts, and expulsions. In the category of expulsions, teen-agers from one-parent homes accounted for 100% of the total number.

These studies and others add to a tradition of research that has focused on a worrisome minority of children who have not fared well during the time of their parents' divorce (Bernard & Nesbitt, 1981). Although fewer studies have been designed to show that divorce has advantages for some children, clinical experience has often led to such a conclusion, and several authors have found it worthwhile to point out these less sensational, although no less dramatic, developments. Boyer (1979) suggested that children of single parents "have highly developed strengths in exploring feelings, evaluating and understanding relationships, skills in managing conflict and mastering disappointments, experience in assuming responsibility, and character traits of independence and resilience" (p. 79). Kurdeck and Siesky (1980) found the attitudes of children aged 5 to 19 toward their parents' divorce to be positive, yet realistic; these children did not seem to view the divorce as a devastating event. Wallerstein and Kelly (1980) offered a normalizing conclusion to their study: "In terms of school success and failure, academic performance of the entire group [five years after parents' divorce] was roughly comparable to what it had been four to five years earlier" (p. 279).

In addition to research and clinicians' opinions that stress either the negative consequences or the growth-producing aspects of divorce for children, increasingly more attention is being given to the intervening variables that seem to contribute to one state or the other. Data support the contention that divorce per se is not the primary variable affecting the success of children in school. For instance, in the Wallerstein and Kelly study (1980), the deterioration of school performance for an extended period of time was very highly correlated with one of two conditions: (1) a seriously disturbed custodial parent, or (2) an erratic, if not a nonexistent relationship with the noncustodial parent (p. 283). The acknowledgment that difficulties arise from variables other than the divorce itself is the only good explanation for the fact that the majority of children of divorce show no signs of prolonged dysfunction.

To summarize evidence to date, divorce is painful, but not psychologically destructive for the majority of children. When compared with children of intact marriages, however, children of divorce are found to be having difficulties in disproportionate numbers. Therefore, although *most* children of divorce make the necessary adaptations, proportionately *more* children of divorce surface with problems.

Family therapists have become more sophisticated about divorce and its many operative variables. Although information is still incomplete, therapists are in a position to help families cope with their children's reactions to divorce. A child's emotional or scholastic dysfunction at school might be due to

1. a predivorce condition
2. a dysfunctional divorce process
3. poor or incomplete parenting before, during, or after divorce
4. benign ignorance on the part of parents or school and, thus, failure to give the child needed support

Well-timed and strategically correct interventions can reverse a child's difficulty.

It is inconsequential whether the family or the school acts first to help the child in distress, but it is best if the family and the school coordinate their efforts. The family therapist can begin by helping parents approach and work with the schools to help their children adjust to the realities surrounding divorce.

WORKING WITH THE FAMILY

Differential Diagnosis of the Family

Before offering guidance to the family of divorce regarding the schools, the family therapist must make an assessment of the family on three very important dimensions: (1) the timing of the initial request for therapy relative to the divorce adjustment, (2) the level of hostility between the parents, and (3) the degree of involvement of each parent with the child's schooling. Graphically, these dimensions fall onto continua as follows:

	PREVENTIVE THERAPY	REMEDIAL THERAPY
TIMING OF INTERVENTION	Predivorce	Postdivorce

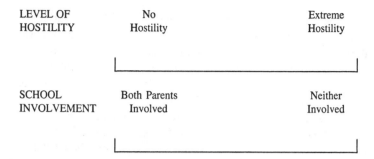

LEVEL OF   No   Extreme
HOSTILITY   Hostility   Hostility

SCHOOL   Both Parents   Neither
INVOLVEMENT   Involved   Involved

Not only do differences in these dimensions dictate different kinds of therapeutic tactics, but also they influence the very nature of therapy itself. With families on the left side of each continuum, the therapist does largely preventive counseling, helping clients foresee difficulties before they arise in order to achieve a "functional divorce." With families on the right side of each continuum, the therapist is most likely to be involved in remedial therapy, helping clients undo errors in judgment or motive within the limits of past events that cannot be reversed.

Timing of the Initial Contact

The earlier the divorcing family contacts the family therapist, the more inclusive the therapist's suggestions can be. If a couple have recently decided to divorce, the therapist can help the couple choreograph their separation to accommodate each parent's need to remain involved in the children's schooling.

After divorce, therapeutic possibilities are limited by the passing of time itself. Routines have been established, and some semblance of stability has been achieved. The therapist must consider these seriously before suggesting a more "progressive" way of doing things that might disrupt a more or less benign peace in the divorced family. Often, stepparents have entered the scene, and they must also be considered as therapy proceeds; their presence sets additional limits, as well as providing additional resources.

Level of Hostility

Regardless of the timing of the initial contact of the family with the therapist, the hostility between the parents dictates many of the therapist's interventions. Although fathers' rights groups have encouraged non-custodial fathers to assert themselves with their ex-wives and with the schools, it is often the school personnel and the child who suffer when a hostile divorce is in process. Many good fathers have opted to forfeit an active involvement in their child's schooling because of the emotional backlash their involvement would cause. Of course, this is not a totally functional arrangement, since the father's input may be invaluable. It may be the best compromise for the daily comfort of the child, however.

When there is virtually no hostility between the parents, the therapist can help the parents consider alternatives far less stereotypic than the divorced family as a one-parent family. The parents can present themselves to the school jointly as they work out the logistics of their divorce and its effect on the child and the school. They can negotiate reasonably to decide who goes to school performances, sports events, and parent conferences.

Level of Involvement

When all other things are under control, parental involvement in a child's schooling is a bonus for the child. When an excessive amount of hostility between parents has been brewing for several years, however, each parent's assertion for equal involvement in the child's schooling can create a nightmarish situation. Under these circumstances, motives for involvement are typically mixed, and not all of them are healthy. Therefore, it is important for the therapist to confront any dysfunctional motives and help parents refocus their attention on what is good for the child.

Sometimes, neither parent is particularly involved with the child's schooling. All the parents' energy seems to be consumed in their own adjustment to the divorce. When this is the case, the therapist should help one or both parents cope better to release some additional "positive energy" and should convince the parent(s) of the importance of supporting the child by becoming involved in the child's schooling. If one parent is having a more difficult time adjusting, the other parent may be able to fill this role. There are many alternative plans if parents and therapist are open to them.

Custody as an Issue

Wallerstein and Kelly (1980) found that many children whose schoolwork deteriorated significantly between 1 year and 5 years after divorce were living with a severely disturbed mother. (All were mothers in this particular study; it is rare for a disturbed father to receive custody of a child.) When a therapist is working with a couple going through divorce, the issue of custody should be raised even if both parents have assumed that custody will fall to the mother. The best compromise for each child should be considered carefully.

When the custodial or would-be custodial parent seems to be psychologically dysfunctional, the issue of custody must be dealt with in therapy. Living with a parent who is unstable is extremely hazardous for children. Of course, under the high stress of divorce, it is difficult to make an accurate assessment of a parent's ability to function. A therapy session is a better place to establish each parent's ability to be the custodial parent than the court is, however. When both parents are able to assume this role, joint custody should be considered seriously. Although joint custody has been viewed with suspicion by many parents, there is increasing evidence that it is worth the logistical problems that come with it (Greif, 1979).

Finally, custody should be considered a renegotiable matter if a child is doing poorly after the divorce. Not only the parent's dysfunction, but also parenting styles and the developmental stage of the child could warrant a change in custody.

Parents' Attitudes toward Divorce and the Schools

Parents commonly believe either that the divorce will automatically devastate and psychologically ruin their children or that their children's resiliency will allow them to survive any and all turmoil without difficulty (Bernard, 1981; Bernard & Hackney, 1983; Sprenkle, 1981). As Hackney (in press) stated, "One might say that crisis (or lack of crisis) is in the eyes of the beholder." Often, parents project their own experience onto their children. If the divorce was their idea, they expect their children to adjust automatically. If, on the other hand, they are devastated by the divorce, they treat their children like fellow victims.

Many of the problems that beset the children of divorce are initiated by parents' attitudes. Therapists should address parental attitudes and attempt to modify them, when necessary. Furthermore, the motivation for certain attitudes should be explored. If a father seems to resist the notion that divorce will *not* ruin his daughter, perhaps he needs to blame the mother for deciding to divorce. Therefore, the daughter's deterioration becomes his trump card.

Attitudes toward the schools must also be addressed in therapy. Divorced parents often feel defensive about their status and project this onto the schools. Many times parents have had unpleasant experiences with a few school personnel and have generalized these to the entire school staff. Again, the therapist must help parents differentiate among erroneous attitudes, those partially based on experience, and those that are realistic and healthy. It is important to point out the effects of these negative and defensive attitudes on the child.

Therapist as Teacher

Divorce counseling is seldom "laid back." Each session is charged with emotion and complicated issues. It is easy for therapists to become enmeshed in weekly crises and neglect to teach their clients some of the current knowledge about divorce. Some therapists regard teaching (i.e., giving information in a direct manner) as contradictory to the role of therapist. This may be true for other types of therapy, but certainly not for divorce counseling. Therapists should have an outline of up-to-date information about the divorce process to distribute to each divorcing client. When school-aged children are involved, this outline should include recent research on the effects of divorce on children.

Teaching is not only the most efficient way to provide important information to parents, but also a method to "ground" parents who are in the throes of their own crisis. Often parents are imprisoned by their emotions, and therapy devoted exclusively to those emotions can reinforce the walls of that prison. Reviewing current thinking regarding divorce is one way to break through the barriers.

Assertiveness Training

It is not uncommon for one parent in a divorcing pair to be unassertive. In fact, many marriage problems may have occurred because one or both spouses were unable or unwilling to assert their rights in a variety of situations. During and following divorce, however, perhaps no other skill serves a parent better in working with the schools than assertiveness. This conclusion is supported by the results of a national survey of single parents and the public schools conducted by the National Committee for Citizens in Education (Clay, 1981). Ricci (1979) also noted that schools react best to the special needs of a child of divorce when the parent is assertive regarding the divorce.

Unfortunately, the parents, particularly the custodial parent, often take a counterproductive stance toward the school by taking offense if the school stereotypes the child or shows insensitivity toward the child, yet doing nothing to inform the school of an impending divorce and the circumstances surrounding the divorce. Wallerstein and Kelly (1980) made the following statement: "It is ironic that at a time in our society when parents increasingly hold the schools responsible for their child's well-being, these same parents fail to provide some of the important tools for the teacher's effective functioning" (pp. 266–267). Accurate and complete information delivered in a nondefensive manner gives school personnel the best opportunity to aid the child in transition.

Because of the well-established pattern of unassertiveness between divorced parents and the schools, it may be necessary for the therapist to coach the parent to be assertive for the sake of the child. Some school systems are easier to approach than others, but a few basic suggestions can be followed by everyone. Among the most obvious is to inform the school administration and the child's teacher of the parents' decision to divorce. A second and more powerful assertion is to approach the school on its policy regarding divorced parents. The custodial parent should let the school know whether he or she wishes the noncustodial parent to be kept informed of the child's school life. This request may also come from the noncustodial parent. The custodial parent who does not want the noncustodial parent to have access to school records must obtain a court order to bar the other parent and present it to the school. In any case, asserting oneself prior to a conflict is far better than waiting for a conflict to occur.

WORKING WITH THE SCHOOL

A working relationship between a family therapist and a school system is still more the exception than the rule. Based on Caplan's (1970) consultation model, most therapist interventions have been client-centered, intended to create positive change for a particular child. Such an intervention is unlikely to lead to any change in the school as a system and is not meant to do so. The more inclusive approaches of consultee-centered (working with school personnel) or program-centered (working with the organizational structure) are needed for broader range change. The level of intervention should be a deliberate decision made by the therapist and the school.

Regardless of the role therapists take with schools, they must be sensitive to the schools' constraints. Some resistance should be expected. Schools feel pressure from society to right many of the wrongs they did not create. Divorce is seen as a case in point. Therapists who wish to work with a school must convince school personnel that they are able and willing to be of service within the confines of the school's restrictions. Therapists must be willing to take time to join with a school as they would do with a family.

Early attempts in the schools to deal with divorce focused on curriculum and programs for children (Bernard, 1978). More recently, administrative policies seem to be the target for change. There is a growing realization that policy statements set a certain tenor within a school, regardless of curriculum. Therefore, one criterion for measuring the success of a family therapist's interventions in the school is the extent to which they influence school policy. Some schools are eager to be influenced; others blindly adhere to the two-parent home as the exclusive model. Any family therapist who works with the schools must be prepared for some failures.

As Ricci (1979) suggested, this is a difficult time for school administrators. The words *mother* and *father* are often replaced by the words *custodial parent, noncustodial parent*, and *stepparent*. Administrators must be comfortable with joint custody, visitation rights, and court orders, which is more than most had bargained for when they began their careers. Therefore, although family therapists can criticize school administrators for resisting change, they must empathize with the plight of these administrators as they walk the tightrope between innovation and tradition. The most important thing is that a growing number of schools are looking for alternatives.

Schools can become more innovative at two levels. They can change *in order to diminish the daily problems* for the school as a consequence of divorce, or they can change *to meet an ideal* of the functional divorce. Although the second level is a more proactive position, the first level of change also requires commitment and cooperation among school personnel.

Most of the daily school problems caused by divorce have to do with an antagonistic relationship between the parents. Many schools have misinterpreted the 1974 Buckley Amendment and have given complete authority over school records to the custodial parent. Even without a court order to justify such action, they have denied the noncustodial parent any information about the child's schooling. Because of this benign (but not excused) ignorance, some schools are facing lawsuits. Similarly, teachers have been asked by the legal representatives of one parent to provide information for use in contested custody cases (Rogers, 1982). Without a school policy on such requests, teachers are left to decide for themselves how to proceed. On a more mundane level, some schools are so unclear on the divorce issue that they do not know whether to ask a noncustodial parent to take a sick child home if the custodial parent cannot be reached.

Schools at the second level of innovation provide leadership for divorcing parents. For instance, schools may establish a policy that all noncustodial parents are to receive the same information that custodial parents receive. They may even have a special parent conference night for noncustodial parents and stepparents, acknowledging the discomfort that keeps many concerned parents away from such conferences. They encourage their staff to stay in touch with parents during the divorce process in order to prevent behavior or academic problems. They communicate to the parents that they *want* the school to be *used* by the child as a support system during this time of transition. Finally, the more innovative schools seek the opinion of divorcing parents as policies are being established.

Because of their familiarity with divorcing families and the issues involved, family therapists are in an excellent position to help schools decide on policy matters. Many schools need this type of input until they become more naturally attuned to the needs of divorcing families and can determine how the schools can assist them in their adjustment to divorce.

AN INTERFACE OF TWO SYSTEMS

From a systemic point of view, both the school and the family function as integral systems. Each has a structure, a set of goals, and a set of guidelines or rules to follow. Given these similarities, the family and the school should be able to comprehend each other and work together toward mutual goals. Under the best of conditions, the school anticipates and facilitates the family system needs as they relate to the child; similarly, the family not only comprehends the school's structure and function, but also coordinates its efforts in a way that aids the child's transition as well as the school's mission.

Unfortunately, this is not often the case. It is more likely that neither the school nor the family comprehends the other's systemic nature. In this case, the natural consequence is that the child is left to interpret each system to the other; however, few children are equipped to accomplish such a mission. Hackney (1981) examined this situation and concluded that "as family and school interface, communication between the two systems becomes an increasingly critical issue so as not to catch the child between competing system loyalties" (p. 53). He also observed that "a crisis occurring within either system will probably be transmitted [through the child] to the other" (p. 51).

The family therapist is ultimately most effective when helping both the family system and the school system to monitor not only the amount of interface between them, but also the quality of that interface. Given the many issues within each system during divorce, it is not surprising that family and school can lose the necessary flexibility in their reactions to each other. The family therapist who can join with each system can facilitate intersystem communication and remove the child from the middle of yet another potential conflict.

REFERENCES

Bernard, J.M. Divorce and young children: Relationships in transition. *Elementary School Guidance and Counseling*, 1978, *12*, 188–198.

Bernard, J.M. The divorce myth. *The Personnel and Guidance Journal*, 1981, *60*, 67–71.

Bernard, J.M., & Hackney, H. *Untying the knot: A guide to civilized divorce*. Minneapolis: Winston Press, 1983.

Bernard, J.M., & Nesbitt, S. Divorce: An unreliable predictor of children's emotional predisposition. *Journal of Divorce*, 1981, *4*, 31–42.

Boyer, S. Tips for working with single parents. *Instructor*, 1979, *89*, 79.

Brown, B.F. A study of the school needs of children from one-parent families. *Phi Delta Kappan*, 1980, *61*, 537 540.

Caplan, G. *The theory and practice of mental health consultation*. New York: Basic Books, 1970.

Clay, P.L. *Single parents and the public schools: How does the partnership work*. Columbia, MD: National Committee for Citizens in Education, 1981.

Elias, M. Tots take the worst blows in divorce. *USA Today*, June 15, 1983, 3D.

Grief, J.B. Fathers, children, and joint custody. *American Journal of Orthopsychiatry*, 1979, *49*, 311–319.

Hackney, H. The gifted child, the family, and the school. *Gifted Child Quarterly*, 1981, *25*, 51–54.

Hackney, H. Children's response to crisis and change. *Early Child Development and Care*, in press.

Kurdeck, L.A., & Siesky, A.E., Jr. Children's perceptions of their parents' divorce. *Journal of Divorce*, 1980, *3*, 339–378.

Ricci, I. Divorce, remarriage, and the schools. *Phi Delta Kappan*, 1979, *60*, 509–511.

Rogers, R. Piggy in the middle. *The Times Educational Supplement*, 1982, 3453: 1753, p. 17.

Snyder, A.A., Minnick, K., & Anderson, D.E. Children from broken homes: Visits to the school nurse. *The Journal of School Health*, 1980, *50*, 186–194.

Sprenkle, D.H. Is there life after divorce? Address delivered at the Purdue University Child and Family Symposium, Spring 1981.

Wallerstein, J.S., & Kelly, J.B. *Surviving the breakup: How children and parents cope with divorce*. New York: Basic Books, 1980.

8. Adlerian Family Therapy

Don Dinkmeyer, PhD
President, Communication and Motivation Training Institute
Coral Springs, Florida

James Dinkmeyer, MA
Associate, Operations Manager, Communication and Motivation
    Training Institute
Coral Springs, Florida

ALFRED ADLER, WHO LIVED AND WORKED IN VIENNA DURING THE first quarter of this century, was one of the first psychologists to emphasize the importance of the family in the development of personality. Adler organized his first child guidance center in 1922; this center was so successful that he opened 27 others (Grunwald & McAbee, in press). These centers were open forums in which Adler encouraged parents, teachers, principals, social workers, and anyone interested in children to participate. Rudolf Dreikurs, a student of Adler's, brought these concepts to the United States, specifically to Chicago, in 1937. He opened centers where he trained counselors from all over the world in Adlerian family counseling (Dreikurs, Corsini, Lowe, & Sonstegard, 1959).

Adlerian family therapy is differentiated from Adlerian family counseling in that

1. all members of the family are usually seen at the same time. If there is a major marital problem, however, the procedure is modified.
2. the session may take from 1 to 1½ hours.
3. the therapist focuses on the psychological movement and the transactions among family members.
4. the therapist has an opportunity to model more active, constructive, and effective behaviors.

We have adapted Adlerian family therapy by adding a planned intervention with an educational component. If the intake procedure reveals that the parents are having significant child-training problems, the parents are asked to come alone to the first interview. At this interview, goals are established and the child-training procedures discussed. The basics of motivating or encouraging children, as well as disciplining children by natural and logical consequences, are presented and discussed. Depending on the age of the children, the parents are asked to read one of the following:

1. *Systematic Training for Effective Parenting* (Dinkmeyer & McKay, 1976)
2. *Systematic Training for Effective Parenting of Teens* (Dinkmeyer & McKay, 1983)
3. *The Basics of Adult-Teen Relationships* (Dinkmeyer, 1976)
4. *The Basics of Parenting* (Dinkmeyer & Dinkmeyer, 1980)

At the ensuing meeting, these concepts are discussed as they apply to specific child-training issues. Depending on the situation and progress being made, the parents may be seen this way for 3 or 4 weeks.

ADLERIAN PSYCHOLOGICAL ASSUMPTIONS

Today's world requires effective interpersonal relationships; social interaction is no longer optional. Since all human movement is guided by subjective goals, it is through influencing this movement and correcting any faulty, mistaken perceptions that therapists can best influence human behavior. Family therapists can teach family members pragmatic procedures for relating to each other. For example, a weekly family meeting or family council provides an opportunity for family members to discuss differences, plan for time together, encourage each other, and deal with any issues (Dreikurs & Soltz, 1964).

Psychological movement is seen in the goal-directed transactions among family members, which reveal, both verbally and nonverbally, the attitudes, beliefs, and values that influence behavior and relationships within the family. Family therapy brings the family together to collaborate with the therapist in identifying common goals. As family members become aware that they have the creative capacity to choose, they are challenged to cooperate.

Congruence occurs when their beliefs, feelings, and actions are in alignment. Congruency enables them to be more caring and concerned. This caring must precede the commitment to change.

ADLERIAN CONCEPTUALIZATION OF THE SYSTEM

In Adlerian psychology, persons are viewed as indivisible, social, decision-making beings whose actions and movements have a purpose (Dinkmeyer, Pew, & Dinkmeyer, 1979). All interactions within the family are interpreted in terms of the purpose of the movement, since movement among family members is guided and motivated by subjective goals. Interactions between family members always makes sense in terms of the social context. By following the sequence of events, the therapist can see the system and the way in which behaviors complement each other.

Joe has learned that he lives in a family whose members bargain. Concerned with control, Joe's father wants Joe to do what he, the father, values. Joe is told that, if he raises his grades to B, he can buy a motorbike, although a motorbike has been considered too dangerous until now. Joe gets the B and receives the bike, but he stops working in school. The method by which both Joe and his father manipulate each other must be discussed.

Behavior has social meaning and a goal, even though its intention may be hidden in nonverbal communication. Family members behave in ways that they believe make them belong or be significant. Any behavior, then, reveals the person's purpose, method of belonging, and striving to be significant. Destructive behavior originated in the context of the group and is best treated within the context of the group. The therapist works to facilitate a reorientation of the passive-destructive goal to an active-constructive goal and to help the person belong in a more cooperative, socially acceptable way. Thus, reorientation may change the desire for attention to involvement, or the desire for power to autonomy.

> Sue challenges the family values at every opportunity. She gets attention and asserts power by staying out too late, refusing to study, or failing to do family chores. This promises to make her parents and her siblings very angry. In a family meeting Sue can learn a more active and constructive way to be powerful. She can not only express her feelings, but also can become involved in determining her own hours and chores.

Adlerians conceptualize the mentally healthy person as one who has social interest, the capacity to give and take in the challenges of life, rather than only self-interest. In a family, social interest involves a feeling of belonging to the family and a desire to cooperate with the family. Social interest and the feeling of belonging are stimulated if the family's communication system is open and there are opportunities for feedback through informal discussions, as well as regular family meetings.

Family Atmosphere

The emotional tone of relationships among family members sets the family atmosphere. Relationships may be autocratic, permissive, or democratic. The therapist and the family collaborate in an investigation of the atmosphere. The investigation is concerned not only with the identified patient and the original reason for therapy, but also with the communication among members of the family. Early in the investigation, the therapist tries to understand the cast of characters, their scripts or lifestyles, and the meaning and messages in the movement among them.

> Jim Sampson is a successful business executive who is accustomed to instantaneous, positive responses and deference. Diane, his wife, has her own social goals and refuses to turn over all decisions to Jim. The boys, Jim, Jr. and Fred, have observed the power struggles and have decided to get their way. Jim, Jr. is stubborn, temperamental, and

challenges all authority. Fred is passive-aggressive, displays inadequacy, and is being excused from tasks. The boys have learned well from their model.

Movement often reveals roles, lifestyles, and the payoff in the transactions. Symptoms and dysfunctional behavior are usually supported by someone in the family. The aggressive adolescent, alcoholic father, or martyred mother play roles that achieve their goals in this setting and provide them with controls and power. The family therapist works to develop relationships of mutual respect in which individuals are treated as equal, responsive, and responsible family members.

Family Constellation

Aware of the influence of the family constellation, the Adlerian family therapist seeks to understand the psychological positions as they affect personalities and communication in the family. The family constellation and birth order are not absolute determiners, but they influence personality. Individuals choose how they will perceive their own position. The personality traits are influenced by age and sex differences. Siblings more than 7 years apart in age do not usually belong in the same psychological constellation. In addition, being an only girl or only boy among members of the opposite sex may make one special.

The first born child may want to remain in a dominant position. The second born often shows a characteristic desire to get ahead or catch up. The second born's personality is influenced by the successes and failures of the first born. The middle child, without the advantages of the first or youngest, tends to feel squeezed and is concerned with fairness. The youngest is never dethroned and, hence, always remains special. This child may become either the most dependent or most successful. The only child never had to struggle for position, may be dependent on parents, and may be insensitive to the needs of others.

The family therapist recognizes the potential characteristics in each position. The challenge is to determine the influence the siblings have on each other and to use this influence to strengthen relationships and increase self-esteem.

Lifestyle

The characteristic pattern that organizes and guides all behavior is the lifestyle. Lifestyle includes the self-concept, the view of the world and human relationships, the goal (guiding self-ideal), and the basic methods for coping with the world. Lifestyle emerges from the experiences in the family atmosphere and family constellation. Parental methods of training also influence the lifestyle, fostering either self-reliant, responsible persons or dependent, insecure persons.

Lifestyles in family therapy are not studied systematically (Dinkmeyer, Pew, & Dinkmeyer, 1979); however, the Adlerian family therapist observes the basic guidelines each person employs for movement within the family, in particular, how each family member faces the challenges of living, how each family member reacts to important family values, and how each family member cooperates with the others to keep the system dysfunctional. The therapist assesses informally the basic theme and lifestyle of each family member. Typical themes include

- "I must be superior."
- "I must please."
- "I must strive to be good."
- "I must be in control."
- "I must hide all mistakes or inadequacies."

The therapist must determine how these themes clash with each other or support each other (e.g., a controller needs a pleaser).

Each person has a goal, for example, to be flawless, to get attention, to be powerful, to be loved, to get more, to get even, to avoid submitting, to avoid functioning, to master everything. The therapist helps family members become aware of their goals through confrontation and tentative hypotheses. Since the goals are chosen, they can be rechosen. The basic purpose of therapy is to help the individual move from destructive goals to constructive goals.

The lifestyle can also be understood in terms of four priorities: (1) comfort, (2) pleasing, (3) control, and (4) superiority. Family members have priorities, as well as goals, for their transactions. The person who seeks comfort provokes irritation and annoyance, while the pleaser may cause others to feel pleased at first, but later exasperated by the pleaser's demands for approval. The controller may seek to control self, others, or situations; in any case, others feel challenged, become tense, and want to resist. The person whose priority is superiority may want to be better, more competent, right, or more useful; such a person may even wish to suffer more nobly as victim or martyr. Others may feel inadequate or inferior.

The feelings evoked by interaction with a person identifies that person's priority. The therapist's sensitivity to the feelings of the target of the transaction and the therapist's experience in this type of transaction help identify the priority in therapy sessions.

THERAPEUTIC APPROACH

Assessment

Before beginning treatment, the therapist must identify goals and priorities that create movement in the family. This can be done by asking simple questions:

- to determine psychological movement in the system, the therapist may ask, "What do you want to happen?" and "What do you hope to accomplish here?"
- to examine perceptions and family dynamics, the therapist may ask, "How does it feel to live in the family?" Varied expectations and goals emerge, which helps clarify the goals and develop cooperative action to free the system.
- to investigate the family system, the therapist may say, "Families operate by rules, but they may not be aware of all the rules. What rules do you think your family operates by?"
- to determine family atmosphere and how each member of the family perceives that atmosphere, the therapist may ask, "How are decisions made in the family—cooperatively or by certain persons?" "Who has the power of control?" "How do they use it?"

The family constellation and the psychological position of the siblings, as well as the ordinal position (order of birth), must be considered by the therapist. The parents influence the behavior and self-esteem of the children, but the siblings also have a very important effect on each other's development and personality. As the therapist observes the interaction and determines who is considered brightest, most cooperative, most rebellious, most sociable, or most responsible, the effect of the family constellation on personality is understood.

Therapeutic Techniques

A variety of techniques are used in Adlerian family therapy.

Understanding. The therapist must help the family to understand the beliefs and perceptions that establish the individual's goals and way of belonging, and influence the psychological movement. Learn to trust primarily psychological movement and to know it reveals intentions and private logic.

Ground Rules for Family Communication. In a family therapy session, the therapist must directly confront dysfunctional communication. The therapist might say, "Jim, I hear you complain about Fred. It would be better to speak directly to Fred than to talk about him." Family members must speak directly to each other, and each person speaks for himself. Family members' communication skills can be improved by providing the direct opportunity to practice communication with each other.

Focus on the Real Issue. Staying out late or homework may seem to be the issue, but the real issue is power or winning. Focusing on the real issue requires the family to confront the choice of changing goals more quickly.

Alignment of Family Goals with Therapeutic Goals. Resistance indicates that the goals of the family members and those of the therapist are not in alignment. If the family and the therapist are working at separate purposes, progress will obviously be impeded. It is necessary to clarify from the beginning what the family members want from therapy and how they expect to get it. Then the therapist should clarify how he or she can help the family reach the goals.

Stimulation of Social Interest. The general goal of Adlerian family therapy is to stimulate cooperation, described by Adler as social interest— the capacity to participate in the give and take of human relationships (Adler, 1938).

Encouragement. An individual's feelings of self-esteem and worth can be increased by encouragement. The therapist encourages by listening, being empathetic, understanding meanings, understanding the system, and identifying and affirming assets and resources. The therapist encourages family members to see perceptual alternatives to the problems challenging them and to focus on any positive intentions and movement (Dinkmeyer & Dreikurs, 1963; Dinkmeyer & Losoncy, 1980; McKay, 1976).

Confrontation of Private Logic, Mistaken Beliefs, and Erroneous Perceptions. Each family member has his or her own view of the world.

Such mistaken beliefs as one must be in control, please others, or always be right bring conflict in family relationships. Until beliefs are changed, behavior does not change.

Sharing of Tentative Hypotheses. The therapist focuses on the underlying intentions or beliefs, tentatively setting them forth for clarification. A tentative hypothesis allows the client to respond instead of defend. If the client rejects the hypothesis, another hypothesis can be formulated jointly. Hypotheses are shared tentatively in the format "Could it be . . .?" or "Is it possible . . .?" with an allusion to the purpose of the behavior.

Paradoxical Intention. Family members may be encouraged to do the very things they claim they want to stop doing (e.g., fighting). They may be asked to fight routinely for 15 minutes, twice a week at a specific time. Thus, the family becomes aware of the ineffectiveness of fighting.

The Change Process

The therapist facilitates the change process through the following cycle:

1. The therapist intervenes with faulty perceptions and beliefs.
2. A support system is developed so people feel they belong and have the courage to try new behaviors. The therapist encourages, values, and emphasizes assets and progress.
3. As individuals communicate and take risks, they are rewarded for their spontaneity and courage by acceptance.
4. As family members have the courage to be imperfect, anxiety and discouragement are decreased and self-esteem and feelings of worth increased.

The therapist helps family members to feel more competent and worthwhile by increasing their social interest (care and concern for each other) and their self-esteem (recognition of the value of their own assets).

As leader of the group, the family therapist helps people to see common problems and deal with all present events by understanding the purpose of the communication and behavior. Family members are then led to process feedback and speak directly, openly, and honestly with each other. Although people may have come to therapy with an implicit agreement to fight and complain, they are helped to make a new decision to cooperate, care, and encourage.

THE FAMILY THERAPIST AND THE SCHOOLS

The Adlerian family therapist works with the schools by investigating with teachers the purpose of problem behaviors in school and alternative ways to motivate and discipline children. The therapist

1. identifies the purpose of any failure to function academically or socially in the schools. The goal or purpose may be a desire for attention, power, revenge, or the display of inadequacy (Dinkmeyer & McKay, 1976).
2. consults with the school staff regarding ways to encourage and discipline the child (Dinkmeyer, McKay, & Dinkmeyer, 1980). The school staff is contacted during the early diagnostic phases, and teachers are encouraged to keep in contact with the therapist by telephone. Such contact helps the therapist to understand movement at school and provides the therapist with an opportunity to help the teachers.
3. helps the family to understand that school is the children's responsibility. The parents assist by setting limits and stimulating general interest in learning, not by doing homework with the child.
4. is available for regular consultation with the school psychologist, school counselor, and teacher.

Family therapy can be related to school problems. It requires the opportunity to speak to the teacher regularly (1) to determine movement and (2) to help the teacher become a therapeutic force. When parents and teachers agree that school is the child's responsibility, conditions for growth are present.

REFERENCES

Adler, A. *Social interest: A challenge to mankind.* London: Faber & Faber, 1938.

Dinkmeyer, D. *The basics of adult-teen relationships (BATR).* Coral Springs, FL: CMTI Press, 1976.

Dinkmeyer, D., & Dreikurs, R. *Encouraging children to learn.* Englewood Cliffs, NJ: Prentice-Hall, 1963.

Dinkmeyer, D., & Losoncy, L. *The encouragement book: Becoming a positive person.* Englewood Cliffs, NJ: Prentice-Hall, 1980.

Dinkmeyer, D., & McKay, G.D. *Systematic training for effective parenting (STEP).* Circle Pines, MN: American Guidance Service, 1976.

Dinkmeyer, D., & McKay, G.D. *Systematic training for effective parenting of teens (STEP/ Teen)*. Circle Pines, MN: American Guidance Service, 1983.

Dinkmeyer, D., McKay, G.D., & Dinkmeyer, D., Jr. *Systematic training for effective teaching (STET)*. Circle Pines, MN: American Guidance Service, 1980.

Dinkmeyer, D., Pew, W., & Dinkmeyer, D., Jr. *Adlerian counseling and psychotherapy*. Monterey, CA: Brooks/Cole, 1979.

Dinkmeyer, D., Jr., & Dinkmeyer, J. *The Basics of Parenting (BOP)*. Coral Springs, FL: CMTI Press, 1980.

Dreikurs, R., Corsini, R., Lowe, R., & Sonstegard, M. *Adlerian family counseling*. Eugene, OR: University Press, University of Oregon, 1959.

Dreikurs, R., & Soltz, V. *Children: The challenge*. New York: Duell, Sloan & Pearce, 1964.

Grunwald, B., & McAbee, H. *Guiding the family: Practical counseling techniques*. Muncie, IN: Accelerated Development, Inc. (in press).

McKay, G. *The basics of encouragement*. Coral Springs, FL: CMTI Press, 1976.

9. Family Therapy for Families with Children Who Have School Behavior Problems: A Social Learning Approach

Arthur M. Horne, PhD
Professor of Counseling Psychology
Indiana State University
Terre Haute, Indiana

John M. Walker
Doctoral Fellow
Indiana State University
Terre Haute, Indiana

The material presented in this article is based, in part, upon the text *Troubled Families: A Treatment Program* by Matthew Fleischman, Arthur Horne, and Judy Arthur, published by Research Press, 1983.

SCHOOL BEHAVIOR PROBLEMS HAVE LONG HAD THE ATTENTION OF family counselors and therapists. In fact, one of the major problems presented to family therapists is the treatment of children with aggressive behaviors. During the 1950s, for example, it was found that nearly two-thirds of all referrals by teachers and parents for mental health services were for children identified as out of control or unmanageable within the school and home (Roach, Gursslin, & Hunt, 1958).

Historically, treatment offered to families for school conduct problems has not always been effective. Furthermore, Bahm, Chandler, and Eisenberg (1961) found that only a small fraction of the children referred for services actually were offered treatment. In his review of family treatment, Levitt (1971) found that, of those who were accepted for treatment, the services offered were generally of a traditional nature and provided little or no help for socially aggressive children. Meltzoff and Kornreich (1970) reported that treatment of individual children by traditional therapy seldom effected lasting change either in the home or in the school; however, studies at that time showed that, if children were not treated at all, their conduct problems tended to continue (Morris, Escol, & Wexler, 1956; Robins, 1966; Zax, Cowen, Rappaport, Beach, & Laird, 1968). Thus, the need for alternative treatment models for aggressive children was evident. Any effective alternative model would have to take into account the family's importance in the development, maintenance, and alteration of disruptive behaviors of children in the home, school, and community.

Social learning is a term applied to the process of people learning from other people and from life experiences. "This learning process takes place within a social environment through observing, reacting to, and interacting with other people; in short, it is an education in human relations" (Fleischman, Horne, & Arthur, 1983, p. 13). Since children are born into a social environment—the family—their behavior patterns are established from their family learning experiences. Applications of social learning theory to family therapy are fairly recent, having developed as a result of carefully controlled studies demonstrating that a social learning approach could be effective with a variety of populations in diverse settings (Bandura, 1969, 1977).

According to social learning theory, those behaviors that are reinforced are more likely to reoccur, and those that lead to punishment are less likely to reoccur. Reinforcement and punishment may occur directly, as they do in operant conditioning models, or they may occur vicariously, as children observe the behaviors of others. Much of an individual's learning occurs not through direct experience, according to social learning theory, but rather through models, observations, and social interaction. Behavior, then, is learned, maintained, and changed through the environment of the individual. In order to influence behavior, the therapist must attend to the physical and social environment, as well as to the cognitions, beliefs, and attitudes of the person. There is a reciprocal interaction between the environment and the individual, with each influencing the other. Similarly, there is a reciprocal interaction among members of families. Family behaviors do not occur in a vacuum, but rather as a complex interaction among the members.

A family generally becomes involved in family therapy because of an identified patient, a target child who has been identified by a parent, teacher, or some other person in the community as disturbed or disruptive. A systems perspective to treating families emerged in the 1950s with the recognition that an individual's behavior cannot be reasonably considered apart from his or her involvement in the family system. Thus, a child's misbehavior is not seen as illogical or crazy, but as a pattern of learned responses to the contingencies of the system in which the child lives. The behavior of others within that system contributes to the individual's deviancy, and the behavior of the individual contributes to and helps maintain the behavior of others toward that person.

Patterson and Hops (1972) postulated that individuals strive to maximize rewards while minimizing costs in their interpersonal relations. Relationships that provide a high proportion of rewards are seen as satisfactory, while those that cost a great deal, personally and emotionally, are seen as unsatisfactory or dysfunctional. Patterson and Hops defined relationships in these terms as either reciprocal or coercive patterns of social interaction. A reciprocal relationship is one in which two people maintain a relationship through the frequent use of mutual positive reinforcement; a coercive relationship is one in which either one or both persons use aversive reactions to control the behavior of the other.

During the 1960s, a number of behavioral treatment programs were developed. For children with school-related problems, in-class treatment programs achieved some success, but improved behaviors were not often maintained. In 1965, since it was recognized that the family plays an important role in determining a child's behavior, Patterson began working with the families of children with school-related problems. His initial work involved treating a single family at a time using such devices as "buzzer boxes" and M&M's candy, but he quickly moved to training parents and others involved in the child's environment to use basic point systems, modeling, time-out, and contingent attention (Patterson & Brodsky, 1966; Patterson, Jones, Whittier, & Wright, 1965; Patterson, McNeal, Hawkins,

& Phelps, 1967). As the model developed, treatment moved from the psychology laboratory to the more naturalistic settings of the school and the home.

In the first large-scale study of the social learning treatment model (Patterson, 1974), 27 boys, aged 5 to 12, were treated in the family context. Approximately two-thirds of the treated boys evidenced at least a 30% reduction in their aggressive behavior, as measured by home observations. Parents reported a 50% reduction in the occurrence of symptoms that concerned them, as measured by a parent daily report form. Follow-up a year later indicated that not only did the improvements persist, but also that siblings' behavior improved, even when the therapist had not extended treatment to the siblings. Therefore, it appeared that parents generalize the skills they learn and use them with other members of the family (Arnold, Levine, & Patterson, 1975).

Research on social learning family therapy has continued. There is now empirical evidence that working with families using this model can be effective (Horne & Van Dyck, 1983) and efficient (Fleischman et al., 1983; Patterson, 1982; Patterson, Reid, Jones, & Conger, 1975).

A TREATMENT MODEL

In the past two decades, several models for treating families with children who exhibit problem behavior have been developed (e.g., Forehand & McMahon, 1981; Patterson et al., 1975; Wahler & Fox, 1980). All the models have similar components, including some form of behavioral assessment, instruction in basic principles of child management, development of a generalization plan, and evaluation of the progress of the family. A treatment overview of a recently published family treatment program adhering to the social learning model is presented in Figure 9-1.

Pretreatment Phase

After the family therapist receives the referral from the school, parent, or some other community source, the appropriateness of treatment is determined. Included in the pretreatment phase is an assessment of the child, to determine the nature and extent of the problem (academic performance, behavioral observations or reports, medical complications). When meeting with the parents to discuss the reason for the referral and the problems experienced, the therapist assesses the parents' resources for working within a treatment program, including work schedules, amount of time with the

Figure 9-1 Treatment Overview

Pretreatment		Intervention				Generalization	Maintenance
Initial Interview Session 1	Setting Up for Success Session 2	Self-Control Session 3	Discipline Session 4	Reinforcement Session 5	Communications Session 6	Generalization Session 7+	Termination and Follow-up
1. Assess the presenting problems and other factors related to participation. 2. Present treatment.	1. Establish treatment goals. 2. Target the problem to work on first. 3. Address setting up conditions and antecedent behaviors related to target behavior.	1. Teach procedures for improving self-management.	1. Select and practice disciplinary response to target behavior.	1. Review concept of reinforcement and implement plan to encourage target behavior.	1. Present basic communication and problem-solving skills.	1. Using a problem-solving approach, assist the family to apply setting up, self-control, discipline, and reinforcement to deal with other concerns. 2. Repeat the above process until remaining concerns are resolved and family's reliance on therapist initiative is reduced.	1. Prepare parents to maintain changes without therapist. 2. Terminate. 3. Offer "booster shots" as needed.

Source: Reprinted with permission from *Troubled Families: A Treatment Program* by M.J. Fleischman, A.M. Horne, and J.L. Arthur. Copyright 1983 by Research Press, Champaign, Ill.

child, their perception of the seriousness of the problem, and any other factors that may affect their ability or willingness to participate in treatment. It is important at this point also to understand the parents' perception of the cause or explanation of the problem (e.g., medical, "He's hyperactive"; biological, "His father's whole family is like this . . . bad genes"; religious, "He's got the devil in him"). It may be decided that, instead of or in addition to family counseling, alternative services are necessary (e.g., marriage counseling for the parents or social services, such as food stamps).

During the pretreatment phase, parents receive an overview of the treatment structure. This includes an explanation to the parents that the therapist will work primarily with them (and with the teacher for school-related concerns), since they spend much more time with the child and can be more effective in changing the child's problem behavior than a therapist who sees the child only 1 hour each week. The therapist should try to develop some optimism in the parents that change can occur. In order to establish a therapeutic alliance with the parents, the therapist must be able to demonstrate effective clinical skills and must not present the program in a mechanistic or rigid fashion.

Upon reaching agreement with the parents to initiate treatment, the therapist contacts the educational personnel involved to inform them of the treatment program and the schedule developed. While teachers and parents usually cite academic or school behavior problems as a major concern, social learning family therapy often begins with problems at home. Generally, parents have little control over the child's school misbehavior when therapy begins, having used their available resources prior to the referral without success. Therefore, the therapist begins by helping the parents gain control over the child's behaviors at home. After they have developed the skills necessary to change the child's behavior at home, they are more likely to have the skills necessary to affect the child's behavior at school by providing consistent consequences, both positive and negative, at home. The child will have learned in the process that the parents are predictable. A relationship develops between the parents and the child founded on trust and caring, which allows the parents to generalize their expectations for positive behavior to the school situation.

Treatment Phase

Setting Up for Success

The second phase of treatment is the intervention phase, which is broken into several parts. The first part, setting up for success, establishes clear treatment goals for the family by means of a goal attainment scaling process (Fleischman et al., 1983). During this time, parents are taught how to work with their child in a way that will be successful. They may be taught to

- rearrange the environment, if necessary (do not take a tired, hungry child on a 3-hour shopping trip; put the stereo out of the reach of curious little fingers)
- develop consistent routines (establish a bedtime routine; schedule a regular family night for fun activities)
- give good, clear commands (get the child's attention; explain exactly what is wanted when and how; tell instead of ask; be firm but polite)
- teach new skills (demonstrate how to do what is expected by breaking it down into small steps, demonstrating, practicing, reinforcing)
- treating each other with more care (treat family members as one would treat a friend or neighbor)
- strengthen marital ties (set aside time for specific activities)
- improve parental coordination (establish ways to agree to disagree that provide consistency for children; divide parenting responsibilities)

Finally, the therapist must encourage parental growth and well-being. Many times, this stage of family treatment produces a great deal of change; the parents begin to interact differently with the children and with each other. The system has changed, and the actors within the system will have to change as well.

Self-Control

It is important for parents to be aware that, if they, as adults, are unable to control themselves, it is not likely that their children will be able to do so either. Poor parental self-control can result in intense, debilitating anger. Parents may become so enraged that they strike out and physically or emotionally abuse the child. Subsequently feeling quite guilty about their treatment of the child, the parents may try to make up for their actions by allowing the child to do or have that which had originally been denied, by buying the child gifts, or by giving special privileges.

Another debilitating emotion is acute depression. Parents often feel that they themselves are out of control, that they are incompetent, and that parenting just is not worth the effort involved. Parents in this frame of mind often let their children do as they wish, with few conditions. This situation then reinforces the parents' notion that they are incapable of effective parenting, which leads to an even more intense depression.

Several methods can be used to teach parents self-control. The importance of effective self-control and problem solving, somewhat along the lines of Glasser's steps of reality therapy (1965), can be taught by having parents learn four basic questions to ask themselves:

1. What is my goal?
2. What am I doing?
3. Is it helping me to achieve my goal?
4. What could I do differently?

Since the parents' goal is an effective and positive relationship with the child and strong anger or depression works contrary to achieving that goal, loss of self-control is not goal-productive.

Parents' faulty thinking patterns are also counterproductive, much as described by Beck (1972), Ellis (1962, 1969), Maultsby (1975), and others. Therefore, the second step of problem solving involves teaching parents how their faulty thinking patterns contribute to their being out of control. Parents are taught a process for establishing calming or goal-oriented thoughts, and a sample thought menu is developed to help them establish a process to move toward more effective control. Another step in the self-control process that parents are taught is relaxation training.

Depending on the age of the child and the type of behavior the child displays, it may be appropriate to teach self-control skills to the child, either individually or in a group through the classroom teacher. Self-control skills for children can be taught by the Turtle Technique, a procedure developed by Schneider and Robin (1976) to help children identify the need for control, learn to relax themselves, and engage in problem-solving activities. Other self-control methods that incorporate cognitive elements into behavioral management are described by Kendall and Hollon (1979) and Meichenbaum (1974, 1977).

Discipline

In the intervention phase of treatment parents are also taught effective disciplinary methods. While many parents receive formal training in their occupational endeavors or even their hobbies, few receive any training in ways to discipline children other than what they themselves experienced as children. The therapist attempts to identify specific correctional procedures that are appropriate for the behavior of the child, presenting them in such a manner that they are understood and usable. As with all phases of social learning treatment, this involves teaching, demonstrating, role playing, and structured practice.

Time Out. Isolating the child for a few minutes after each instance of misbehavior deprives the child of social interaction—reinforcement. The child learns through time out that the misbehavior results in not receiving the attention that the behavior previously elicited.

Grandma's Law. A nonconfrontative procedure, Grandma's law is to let the child know that the desired behavior (do homework) must be completed before the child is able to engage in the activities he or she wishes (watch television).

Natural and Logical Consequences. Particularly appropriate for children who act helpless or irresponsible is the use of natural and logical consequences. The child who, for example, fails to come to dinner when called suffers the consequence of having no dinner for the evening. The child who forgets a bathing suit sits by the shore while the other family members swim.

Withholding Attention. The procedure that works best for small children who whine, pout, pretend to cry, and in other ways pester adults for attention is to withhold attention.

Withdrawal of Privileges. When a child tests the parents' willingness to use the other disciplinary procedures, there must be a backup. Taking away privileges is an especially appropriate correctional procedure for older children (if you are not home from school by 4:30, there will be no telephone privileges tonight). The withdrawal of fewer privileges for a short period of time is more effective than the removal of major privileges for great lengths of time.

Assignment of Extra Work. When the behaviors to be remedied include more serious offenses, such as lying, stealing, damaging property, and school problems, assigning extra work around the home can be effective.

Reinforcement

After family members have demonstrated mastery of correctional procedures, they are taught reinforcement methods. In teaching reinforcement, the therapist again presents parents with ideas that have been proved successful over time. The parents must understand that the procedures work when presented consistently and when the goal of the family is to have more positive reciprocal interactions.

Social Reinforcement. Verbal messages (e.g., compliments, thanks), physical contacts (e.g., hugs, smiles, kisses), or other social attention that strengthens the desired behaviors comprise social reinforcement. The parents are taught that social reinforcement should be given as soon as possible after an event has occurred, that appropriate behavior can be maintained with continued social reinforcement, and that social reinforcement alone may not be an adequate incentive to change.

Formal Reinforcement. While social reinforcement is desirable, formal reinforcement is often required to maintain desired behaviors. For example, a point system may be used in which the child earns points each day for particular behaviors that are desired, such as making the bed, picking up the room, and feeding the cat. An allowance contingent on certain behaviors is generally more effective with older children. A third form of formal system is contracting, in which the parent agrees to do something pleasant for the child in return for desired behaviors.

Communication

While all families communicate, dysfunctional families do not know how to communicate in a way that develops positive reciprocal relationships. Instead, coercive, painful interactions are generally the rule. While all therapeutic steps involve communications skills for families, parents are very carefully taught during the communications stage of the intervention phase specific ways to communicate with their children in a positive, effective manner. Parents learn to deliver messages nonverbally and verbally in such a manner that the messages are likely to be received well and understood; they also learn active listening skills. Communication patterns to be avoided are also discussed. While the child may be involved in any of the sessions, depending on the age and cooperativeness of the child, it is especially useful to have the child present when communications skills are being taught so that the therapist can accurately assess the family's ability to use the skills being taught.

Generalization

During the generalization phase, parents begin to use the skills they have developed and generalize these skills to other situations. At this point, active school intervention procedures begin. The therapist meets with the parents and any school personnel involved to work out a plan of treatment that builds on the changes already established in the home treatment. After school officials have been informed of the progress made by the parents in the home, goals are developed for the child around school activities and behaviors. The desired behaviors are carefully described and a daily report card is developed (Fleischman et al., 1983). The daily report card lists the desired behaviors (e.g., attends to and stays on task, works independently, completes and turns in assignments) and the period of time for which the activities are expected (e.g., 8 to 10 A.M., 10 to 12 A.M.) or the subjects for which the activities are expected (e.g., reading, arithmetic, social studies).

The daily report card is explained to the child. Each day, the teacher takes the card and checks off whether the desired behavior occurred. If it did, the parents provide a positive consequence at home. If the behavior did not occur, the parents provide a disciplinary activity and have the child complete any work not finished at school.

The school intervention program takes very little teacher time and effort, particularly when compared with the time and effort required to discipline a misbehaving child. When implementing the program, teachers must be aware that positive change is expected and has occurred in the home (developing a positive set). Furthermore, teachers must know that they have the full cooperation of the parents. The teacher may need some direct assistance in teaching style or methods, disciplinary activities for the classroom, self-control skills for children, or other methods of support. It may be best to seek the support from within the school system in order to avoid any suggestion that the therapist lacks confidence in the educational system. If the school requests consultation on classroom management and teaching skills and that area is within the repertoire of the therapist, it may be given. Otherwise, school personnel or other consultants should be made available to the teacher.

OTHER CONSIDERATIONS

The model presented may be used by therapists in community mental health settings, by private practitioners, by social agency personnel, or by school personnel. One school district provides elementary counselors for schools, and the counselors provide the treatment described as a part of their community offering through the school.

While the model presented follows a somewhat structured format, it is not rigid. There is flexibility, depending on the applications made by the user. As a result of using the program, the entire family is expected to change. The program is not designed to get children to conform; rather, the goal is to change coercive family processes to positive interactions.

REFERENCES

Arnold, J., Levine, A., & Patterson, G.R. Changes in sibling behavior following family intervention. *Journal of Consulting and Clinical Psychology,* 1975, *43,* 683–688.

Bahm, A.K., Chandler, C., & Eisenberg, L. *Diagnostic characteristics related to service on psychiatric clients for children.* Paper presented at the Thirty-Eighth Annual Convention of Orthopsychiatry, Munich, Germany, 1961.

Bandura, A. *Principles of behavior modification.* New York: Holt, Rinehart & Winston, 1969.

Bandura, A. *Social learning theory.* Englewood Cliffs, NJ: Prentice-Hall, 1977.

Beck, A.T. Phenomena of depression: A synthesis. In D. Offer & D. Freedman (Eds.), *Modern psychiatry and clinical research: Essays in honor of Roy S. Grinker, Sr.* New York: Basic Books, 1972.

Ellis, A.A. *Reason and emotion in psychotherapy.* New York: Stuart, 1962.

Ellis, A.A. A cognitive approach to behavior therapy. *Interactional Journal of Psychotherapy,* 1969, *8,* 896–900.

Fleischman, M.J., Horne, A.M., & Arthur, J.L. *Troubled families: A treatment program.* Champaign, IL: Research Press, 1983.

Forehand, R.L., & McMahon, R.J. *Helping the noncompliant child.* New York: Guilford Press, 1981.

Glasser, W. *Reality therapy.* New York: Harper & Row, Colophon, 1965, 1975.

Horne, A.M., & VanDyck, B. Treatment and maintenance of social learning family therapy. *Behavior Therapy,* in press.

Kendall, P.C., & Hollon, S.D. *Cognitive-behavioral interventions: Theory, research, and procedures.* New York: Academic Press, 1979.

Levitt, E.E. Research on psychotherapy with children. In A.E. Bergin & S.L. Garfield (Eds.), *Handbook of psychotherapy and behavior change.* New York: John Wiley, 1971.

Maultsby, M.C., Jr. *Help yourself to happiness.* New York: Institute for Rational Living, 1975.

Meichenbaum, D. *Cognitive-behavior modification.* Morristown, NJ: General Learning Press, 1974.

Meichenbaum, D. *Cognitive-behavior modification.* New York: Plenum Press, 1977.

Meltzoff, J., & Kornreich, M. *Research in psychotherapy.* New York: Atherton Press, 1970.

Morris, H.H., Jr., Escol, P.J., & Wexler, R. Aggressive behavior disorders of childhood: A follow-up study. *American Journal of Psychiatry,* 1956, *112,* 991–997.

Patterson, G.R. Interventions for boys with conduct problems: Multiple settings, treatments, and criteria. *Journal of Consulting and Clinical Psychology,* 1974, *42,* 471–481.

Patterson, G.R. *Coercive family process.* Eugene, OR: Castalia, 1982.

Patterson, G.R., & Brodsky, G. A behavioral modification programme for a child with multiple problem behaviors. *Journal of Child Psychology and Psychiatry,* 1966, *7,* 277–295.

Patterson, G.R., & Hops, H. Coercion, a game for two: Intervention techniques for marital conflict. In R. Ulrich & P. Mountjoy (Eds.), *The experimental analysis of social behavior.* New York: Appleton-Century-Crofts, 1972.

Patterson, G.R., Jones, R., Whittier, J., & Wright, M.A. A behavior modification technique for a hyperactive child. *Behavior Research and Therapy,* 1965, *2,* 217–226.

Patterson, G., McNeal, S., Hawkins, N., & Phelps, R. Reprogramming the social environment. *Journal of Child Psychology and Psychiatry,* 1967, *8,* 181–195.

Patterson, G.R., Reid, J.B., Jones, R.R., & Conger, R.E. *A social learning approach to family intervention* (Vol. 1). Eugene, OR: Castalia, 1975.

Roach, J.L., Gursslin, O., & Hunt, R.G. Some social-psychological characteristics of a child guidance clinic caseload. *Journal of Consulting Psychology,* 1958, *22,* 183–186.

Robins, N.L. *Deviant children grown up: A sociological and psychiatric study of sociopathic personality.* Baltimore: Williams & Williams, 1966.

Schneider, M., & Robin, A. The turtle technique: A method for the self-control of impulsive behavior. In J. Krumboltz & C. Thorensen (Eds.), *Counseling methods.* New York: Holt, Rinehart & Winston, 1976.

Wahler, R.G., & Fox, J.J. Solitary toy play and time out: A family treatment package for children with aggressive and oppositional behavior. *Journal of Applied Behavior Analyses,* 1980, *13,* 23–39.

Zax, M., Cowen, E., Rappaport, J., Beach, D., & Laird, J. Follow-up study of children identified early as emotionally disturbed. *Journal of Consulting and Clinical Psychology,* 1968, *32,* 369–374.